SCARS

SCARS

AMERICAN POETRY
IN THE FACE OF VIOLENCE

EDITED BY
CYNTHIA DUBIN EDELBERG

THE UNIVERSITY OF ALABAMA PRESS
TUSCALOOSA AND LONDON

BOOK AND COVER DESIGN BY ERIN TOPPIN BRADLEY

COVER ILLUSTRATION COPYRIGHT © 1995 DANA TAYLOR LONES
USED BY PERMISSION.

∞

The paper on which this book is printed
meets the minimum requirements of American
National Standard for Information Science-Permanence
of Paper for Printed Library Materials, ANSI Z39.48-1984.

95 96 97 98 99 00 01 02 03 04 — 10 9 8 7 6 5 4 3 2 1

Library of Congress Cataloging-in-Publication Data

Scars : American poetry in the face of violence / edited by
    Cynthia Dubin Edelberg.
        p.   cm.
    ISBN 0–8173–0787–7 (alk. paper)
    1. Violence — Poetry.   American Poetry.
I. Edelberg, Cynthia Dubin, 1940–
PS595.V55S33   1995
811.008'0355—dc20   95-2952

British Library Cataloguing-in-Publication Data available

IN MEMORY OF DAVID DUBIN

FOR STU

CONTENTS

II. VIOLENCE AND RACE

III. THE SCARS OF WAR

PREFACE

This collection of fifty-nine poems by contemporary American poets is devoted to the many manifestations of violence to be found in American society today.

I have selected poems from experience, poems often hard-hitting and ruthless in their honesty, while avoiding the sensational and the bizarre. There are no larger-than-life psychopaths, serial killers, or mass murderers here—they would distract from the horror of more "mundane" violations. Rather, the poems in this anthology bear witness to the mental and physical abuse suffered by women and children, the violence of racism in all its subtle and not-so-subtle forms, and the experience of ordinary men forced to contend with the violence of war. Such poems of accusation, only recently accepted into the mainstream of American poetry, give voice to these often hidden forms of violence and exploitation. The poems are straightforward, unflinchingly graphic, and accessible. Driven by the pain and bitterness of experience, these poems demand the sympathetic attention of their readers.

The anthology is divided thematically into three distinct sections. Part I offers poems reacting to violence in the domestic sphere. Part II provides a wide variety of poems protesting racial violence, mostly written by Native-American, African-American, Latino, and Asian-American poets. Part III offers a backward glance at the experiences and effects of combat in World War II, and during the wars in Korea and Vietnam.

The impulse for assembling this collection came from my study of American war poetry from the American Revolution to Vietnam. I found in American war poetry a natural and recurrent fascination with violence. I became interested in the idea that most of these poets seemed to agree that wartime violence is simply a continuation of other kinds of violence perpetuated by civilians against civilians during intervals of peace. Although there seems to be "a level of violence built into the planet," as A. R. Ammons says, in the last few years many who have long believed public complaint was pointless have come to see the potential power of their combined voices. Poetry's chief value in the face of violence is, at the very least, to stand as a testament to what has actually happened; however, I hope that the poems in this collection can also serve as a force for change—that the relative safety of vicarious experience will help to break down the barriers to confrontation and action.

CYNTHIA EDELBERG

ACKNOWLEDGMENTS

I am indebted to all the contributors for their confidence, sustained enthusiasm, and generosity. Rachel Blau DuPlessis and Pamala Karol made valuable and timely suggestions. Marion Root solved all the disk problems and David Dubin critiqued the entire manuscript. And to my closest friends, for love: my husband Stuart Edelberg and our children, Wendy, Jacqueline and Andrew, Helen and Jay.

SCARS

I. DOMESTIC VIOLENCE

"I wish I could tenderly lift from the dark side of history, voices that are anonymous, slighted—inarticulate."

—SUSAN HOWE

from "There Are Not Leaves Enough to Crown to Cover to Crown to Cover"

ALBERT GOLDBARTH
Of Ontology

The bruises are beautiful really: orchid, plum, bordeaux.
We need them. These are the overlush flowers of blood we bid
float broken through our pale skins when talk of divorce gets
physical and drunk. And we need that talk—that pain
in the range of our comprehension. There are other flowers,
lichen smears, that live off rock and height, at the unthinkable
line where planet ends and God's ordered heavens begins,
if there's a God and if there's order in that frightening foulard
of dark and crucible-fires up there . . . no wonder

we choose familiar hurt. At times I've known it sure
as anyone: that August at the beach, when we were
reaching the final weeklong-held cacophony-note in a year
of absolutely wounding squabble . . . at the edges where
our love-stuffed suffering stopped, there was a silence
so articulate in describing ideas of entropy,
malignant tumors milktooth-sized, oblivion and chance,
we'd hear it in between two waves and redouble
our pots-and-pans duet of damaging clamor. And

M. and C., who lug their dead marriage to parties, the
better to raise its rich, pit-retch dissection-stink in public.
And H., her fist all night at her father's fat door, come
out you sonofabitch come out, all night until
the cops squealed up in that earliest, watery dawn
when the sky is like fluid leaked from a clubbed fish.
And W., quit his 6-figure job, bummed freights,
settled down with his ex, left, took a male lover,
left, returned to his bigtime exec desk, quit . . . Each,

a bruise. And some are canned-peas-green with
swine's-eye-pink mottled into the center. And some
are mulberry-blue with carnelian shot through. And one is a
perfect coal-and-indigo feather fit in skin
the unspeakably delicate ivory color of first tusk . . .
Each, a sweet, diversionary trauma. Kings
don't war for beds of gold-and-pearl, a king once said:
they war to keep their beds from floating into the soul-eating
emptiness between stars. One night I woke

inside an August after-midnight where the waters ditto
those sparks in the sky so truly, there's no up or down and living is
being lost in space. I slipped our wicker bed and walked the sands
where we were also roughly repeated: some young couple,
"you did," "I didn't," "you sure the fuck did"—they hugged
that bicker to their chests like blankets fighting cold.
Eventually, I even heard some slaps. And so they had them
then—a small bouquet of bloodflowers
rooting them, naked and obdurate, into the here-and-now. And

of course the opposite happens. The sun was naked burning.
At noon, some guy sprawled flat on a dune
and started talking to the air. To the column of air
he was the base for, talking all the way to whatever conceptual
cornicework of the universe he held up. I could see,
it was easy, he'd been hurt in love—sexual or parental or
who-knows-what-or-why, but hurt. From too much of this world.
He was spreadeagled, open, he deliquesced like a tablet
so happily into the wide, light fields of ontology.

HARVEY SHAPIRO
How Many Times

How many times
Can you go back to the same spot
With love? I never hope to know.
We work patiently at our quarrels,
Starting them now like love,
Deliberately but with elaborate
Ease. When they catch
We marvel at the blaze,
Crowding in close.
"Inexhaustible!" we shout at one another,
Happy for the moment.
I never hope to know
How many times.

JANICE MIRIKITANI

Autumn Comes

Autumn comes
like a buyer of cloth,
her long fingers
touching,
turning orange,
yellow, brown.

taking what she wants,
stretching
the bone taut air.

Her skin crackles beneath
our feet.

        I didn't think anyone wanted me,

bruises pulled
like a sweater around
my neck.

We talk
in the pore tightening air,
branches bare,
about the girl buried in the chill
of prewinter.

We show each other
our mutilated children
in the guise of women
as autumn plucks
at our lips.

Each color,
blue, black, ochre
popping like kisses

on the rib lined flesh,
the puberty soft thighs.

And we muse
how women
keep bruises
hidden
beneath dead
leaves.

BRUCE WEIGL
For the Wife Beater's Wife

With blue irises her face is blossomed. Blue
Circling to yellow, circling to brown on her cheeks.
The long bone of her jaw untracked
She hides in our kitchen.
He sleeps it off next door.

Her chicken legs tucked under her
She's frantic with lies, animated
Before the swirling smoke.
On her cigarette she leaves red prints, red
Like a cut on the white cup.
Like a skin she pulls her sweater around her.
She's cold,
She brings the cold in with her.

In our kitchen she hides.
He sleeps it off next door, his great
Belly heaving with booze.
Again and again she tells the story
As if the details ever changed,
As if blows to the face were somehow
Different beating to beating.

We reach for her but can't help.
She retreats into her cold love of him

And looks across the table at us
As if across a sea.
Next door he claws out of sleep.
She says she thinks she'll do something
After all, with her hair tonight.

JANICE MIRIKITANI
Healthy Choices

Hold still

Keep quiet.

Get a degree
to learn how to talk
saying nothing.

Catch a good man
by being demure.
the one your mother chooses.

Let him climb you
whenever his urge,
amidst headaches
and menstrual aches
and screaming infants.
And when he bids
quick, turn over.

Hold still.

Make your tongue
a slab of cement
a white stone etched
with your name.
Kill your stories with knives

and knitting needles
and Clorox bleach.

Hide in your mysteriousness
by saying nothing.

Starch your thoughts
with ironed shirts.

Tie your anger
with a knot in
your throat
and when he comes
without concern
swallow it.

Hold still.

Keep desire
hopeless as ice
and sleepless nights
and painful as a pinched eyelid.

Keep your fingers
from the razor,
keep your longing
to sever
his condescension
safely in your douchbag.

Turn the blade
against yourself.
Don't twitch
as your slashed wrists
stain your bathroom tiles.
Disinfect with Pine Sol.

Hold still.

Keep quiet.

Keep tight your lips,
keep dead your dreams,
keep cold your heart.

Keep quiet.

And he will shout
praises
to your
perfection.

RACHEL BLAU DUPLESSIS
Medusa

1.

Flat-faced   cave-space
splay eye   see
fat mulch   intertwy
canna say

Bare as a veld   a Welt
crosst tongue speak it
too out too dumb
pock muck.

To which
he held the meanings up
a silver quick shield slick
shimmer

showing which
is object, which subject,
the discourse
faceting her.

She is the thing he
flickers with his light.
She sees it
thru his eyes

her days thru his rays
her face thru his orbs
her phase thru his eye-
balls.

Her he can and as he can
he ken and names the
knowing;
breaks her

in
to being ridden,
over the half-spoken,
over the forgotten.

2.

Ever who
is seed
astride me
ken can word ran
sharp honed

over my
mutter-
ring
unwitting.

Everywhere
I see
inside me
Man
poised

on my eye
a knife
ceaselessly
on a whetstone.

3.

White slice thru tree
thru earth, sky

forcing the branch
ripping the tree.

It is like this:

Dirt
in my brain

over and over
dirt in my brain.

4.

A cave of pain   a howling mouth

It is
                dark
                        the emptied self

Striking my head on the rock my mother

5.

Stole
they
eye of my mother,
stole they teeth,
mother.

Broke the moon box
where she keep
the deep socket
of the child set solid.

Whole bright
tooth bone
Round gnawing
eye stone.

Stole
they
eye of my mother,
stole they teeth,
mother.

Eye-tooth
tooth-eye
cavern slug
hair-face

she weave a woven
to webble the wobble words.
A-
gnomy
hey nonny nonny.

But stole
the shuttle eye
from my mutter
her loopy threads
tho he has wise

stole the teeth out
of my mutter
her pearly seeds
tho he has knives.

6.

What is this thing
this ancient middenstead?
All stark.

It is a stone.
Its lips are stone.
Its eyes are mica mirrors.

It stands; states
I am the crossroad
stone.

7.

What grow
growns roots out.
What grow roots
crown down web
listen root.

What grow
know spout out.
What grow vine
writhe listen long
voice sprout.

What grow
wide hair weed.
What grow slimy
lithe hum tide
loosy grewn hair.

O voice seed.
Listen root.
Spring sprout.
Head web.

From the eye jet
from the tooth debt
rock and reck
rock and reckon.

8.

Tunnel black mouth
screams in the open
Propulsive echo-long
howl from my own tunnel
Resounding in the round tunnel
I have unburied.
I wrench the root cord.

With every thick stone split
a knotty pulp
root-rattle, stem-snattle
corona open(r)ing
in the cave-heavy corridor.
Roots up!   Rouse up!
It shoots out from inside.

Ten hundred heads blood-rich from mine
my lava head, my rocky mine.
The sprout the burst the leap
of sight
the spurt the spoke the ken
of voice

in sight, my netted reach
in voice, my knotted speech.

JANICE MIRIKITANI
Without Tongue

The sun stood among corn, dead in summer.
Dust whirlwinding off dry fields.
He had awoken her for the last time,
burying his head into her shoulder, clawing
open her thighs like the wide branches of stone pine.
She lay, passive, as always. Breathless. Without tongue,
a dead boat on the bottom of the sea,

a wingless beetle waiting for descending shoe.
She dresses. Walks to the meadow shaded
with hawthorne, oak, white birch.
She lifts the rock where she had buried the knife,
afraid she would use it to kill her father.
Her tongue tastes its cold steel edge,
shrill like blood.
She returns to her kitchen, water steaming
in the kettle. Prepares tea
with leaves of shiso no ha, soaked in kyoto plum
and salt. Dried. Sweet bitterness on her tongue.
Chinese flowers bloom in her throat.
She cleans the blade and returns it to the drawer.

AMY CLAMPITT
Meridian

First daylight on the bittersweet-hung
sleeping porch at high summer; dew
all over the lawn, sowing diamond-
point-highlighted shadows;
the hired man's shadow revolving
along the walk, a flash of milkpails
passing; no threat in sight, no hint
anywhere in the universe, of that

apathy at the meridian, the noon
of absolute boredom; flies
crooning black lullabies in the kitchen,
milk-soured crocks, cream separator
still unwashed; what is there to life
but chores and more chores, dishwater,
fatigue, unwanted children; nothing
to stir the longueur of afternoon

except possibly thunderheads;
climbing, livid, turreted alabaster
lit up from within by splendor and terror
—forded lightning's
                    split-second disaster.

ROBERT WRIGLEY
The Creche

It survived the loud, jostling train
from Baden to Berlin, and the heave
and slant, the pitch, pivot and lean
of the bad boat to New York.
She held it to her in a hatbox
stuffed with husks, all across steerage
and Pennsylvania, down the slow road
of the Ohio River to Cairo
and up the dirt tracks and coal-
paved paths to Frankfort, Illinois,
her sudden husband, her life.
She was mined for the children
in her, one daughter, then another,
a short seam, quick to clay,
and not a single son to save them.

But each December found her unfolding
from their sheaths the pale
figures from Dresden: Holy Mother, mild
worker in wood, stock reclined
and ruminant, the infant peering skyward
through His upheld hands. And through the years
we have come to know this story,
how starved, buried on scrip to the company store,
the miner came coal-hearted home,
winter just begun, his daughters already asleep,
and the creche below a sprig of pine.
How blind in the peripheral light, unhelmeted
to rage, he crushed the manger and the tiny Lord
in his blackened right hand,
spat the word *woman* in her face,
and left that night and never returned.

There the story ends, but for one daughter
who married, bore another, who bore
a son, who fathered three boys—two that survived—
and one that passed on the creche,
the Holy Mother, husband, endlessly
sleepy stock, and the gap since then gathered round,

its eloquent absence,
its grip more powerful than any man's.

MAXINE KUMIN
Leisure

The seldom-traveled dirt road by their door
is where, good days, the Scruffses take their ease.
It serves as living room, garage, *pissoir*
as well as barnyard. Hens scratch and rabbits doze
under cars jacked up on stumps of trees.

Someone springs for a dozen bottles of beer.
Someone tacks a target to a tire
across the road and hoists it seductively
human-high. The Scruffses love to shoot.
Later, they line the empty bottles up.

The music of glassbreak gladdens them. The brute
sound of a bullet widening a rip
in rubber, the rifle kick, the powder smell
pure bliss. Deadeyes, the Scruffses lightly kill.

Self-fulfilling Prophecy

If Lonnie Scruffs comes back, he's guaranteed
free room and board in the State's crowbar hotel.
His girlfriend Grace, a toddler at her heels
and in her arms a grubby ten-month jewel,
looks to be pregnant again. Not his seed.
It's rumored this one was sired by his dad.

Towheads with skyblue eyes, they'll go to school
intermittently, learn how to read,
be mocked, kept back or made to play the fool
and soon enough drop out. Their nimble code,
hit first or get hit, supplants the Golden Rule.

It all works out the way we knew it would.
They'll come to no good end, the Scruffses' kids.

ALICIA OSTRIKER

The Boys, The Broomhandle, The Retarded Girl

Who was asking for it—
Everyone can see
The facts in the oak and plaster courtroom,
Beneath the coarse flag draped
There on the wall like something on a stage
Which reminds her of the agony of school
But also of a dress they let her wear
To a parade one time,
Anyone can tell
She's asking, she's pleading
For it, as we all
Plead—
Chews on a wisp of hair,
Holds down the knee
That tries to creep under her chin,
Picks at a flake of skin, anxious
And eager to please this scowling man
And the rest of them, if she only can—
Replies *I cared for them, they were my friends*

It is she of whom these boys
Said, afterward, *Wow, what a sicko,*
It is she of whom they boasted

As we all boast, as we reach
Across that oaken bench to touch for luck the flag
Hung in law's house, and avoid
Touching the girl.

SHARON OLDS
Leaving the Island

On the ferry on the last morning of summer, a
father at the snack counter deep in the boat gets
breakfast for the other up on deck, a
man with a long sunburned nose so
pointed it pulls his upper lip
away from his teeth with the force of its thrust, its
yearning forward, a man with a bent
wavy band of hair combed across his
bald spot like a silver ribbon
laid on his head. *Here, let me drink some of*
Mom's coffee so it won't be so full
for you to carry, he says to his son,
a dark-haired boy of twelve. The boat lies
lower and lower in the water as all the
cars drive on, it tilts its massive
gray floor like the flat world.
I pay for my tea and walk away and
then it starts, the screaming at the side of the
room, *I carry four things*
and I only give you one, and you drop it,
what are you, a baby? A high male
scream, and it doesn't stop, *Are you two?*
Are you a baby? I give you ONE THING,
no one in the room moving, a slow
steaming pool spreading on the floor, little
sea with its own waves at the edges as the
ferry shifts, the boy standing at the
shore of it, rigid. *Can't you do anything*
right? Are you two? Are you two? the piercing
cry of the father. *Go away,*
go up to your mother, get out of here—
the purser calmly swabbing the floor, the
coffee rushing up easily into the mop,
the father leaving the room, the boy not
moving from where the first scream touched him

and I could not just walk past him, I paused and
said, *I spilled my coffee on the deck, last trip, it*

happens to us all: He turned to me a
face of disgust, everting his lips so the
gums gleamed, he hissed a low
guttural dark gagging hiss, the
noise a cornered animal makes, a
trapped bat baring its teeth and
rolling thick spit on its palate as a warning, he
stood at the edge of the mopped stain, that
glazed shape like a continent, and in a
voice like Gollum's or the *Exorcist* girl when she
made that stream of vomit and beamed it
eight feet straight into the minister's mouth
he said *Shut up Shut up Shut up,*
protecting his father, peeling from himself a
fine wing of hate and wrapping it
tightly around the father and son
like an angel shielding them.

GERALD STERN
The Bull Roarer

I

I only saw my father's face in butchery
once—it was a horror—there were ten men
surrounding a calf, their faces were red, my father's
eyes were shining; there might have been fewer than ten,
some were farmers, some were my father's friends
down from the city. I was nine, maybe eight;
I remember we slept a few hours and left
at four in the morning, there were two cars, or three,
I think it was West Virginia. I remember
the pasture, the calf was screaming, his two eyes
were white with terror, there was blood and slaver
mixed, he was spread-eagled, there was a rope
still handing from his neck, they all had knives
or ice picks—is that possible?—they were beery,
drunk, the blood was pouring from the throat

but they were stabbing him, one of them bellowed
as if he were a bull, he was the god
of the hunters, dressed in overalls and boots,
the king of animals; they seemed to know—
some of them seemed to know—the tendons and bones,
they were already cutting and slicing, pulling
the skin off, or maybe that was later, I stood there
staring at them, my father with a knife;
we didn't even have a dog—my mother froze
whenever she saw one—we were living in Beechview,
we had the newest car on the street, it was
an ugly suburb, everything was decent,
there was a little woods, but it was locust,
it would be covered with houses, we didn't even have
a parrot, my father left at eight in the morning
and drove his car downtown, he always wore
a suit and tie, his shoes were polished, he spent
the day with customers, he ate his lunch
at a little booth, I often sat with him,
with him and his friends, I had to show off, I drew
their likenesses, I drew the tables and chairs,
it was the Depression, none of them had brass rings
hanging from their ears, they all wore socks,
and long-sleeved shirts, they ate and drank with passion.

II

My mother is eighty-seven, she remembers
the visit to the farm, there was her brother,
my uncle Simon, and there was his friend, MacBride,
Lou MacBride, he was the connection, he was
a friend of the farmer's, maybe a cousin. I asked her
about the killing—"that is the way those farmers
got their meat, they lived like that, they butchered
whatever they needed." I asked if she could remember
anything strange, was she nervous or frightened?
"There was the tail, they cut the tail off
and chased each other; it was like pinning the tail
to the donkey." Both of us laughed. I didn't have the heart
to mention my father's face, or mention the knife—
and, most of all, my pain. What did I want?

That he should stay forever locked inside
his gold-flecked suits? That he should get up in the dark
and put his shoes on with a silver knife?
That he should unbutton his shirts and stuff the cardboard
into a chute? That he should always tie
his tie with three full loops, his own true version
of the Windsor knot? And what did I want for myself?
Some childish thing, that no-one would ever leave me?
That there would always be logic—and loyalty?
—I think that tail goes back to the Paleolithic.
I think our game has gory roots—some cave,
or field, they chased each other—or they were grimmer,
pinning that tail, some power was amassed,
as well as something ludicrous, always that,
the tail was different from the horns, or paws,
it was the seat of shame—and there was envy,
not just contempt, but envy—horns a man has,
and he has furry hands and he has a mane,
but never a tail. I remember dimly
a toy we had, a kind of flattened stone,
curved at the sides, with a long rope at one end
we whirled around to make a thundering noise.
This was a "bull-roarer"; we made thunder
and felt the power in our shoulders and legs.
I saw this toy in southern Italy;
I saw children throwing it over their heads
as if they were in central Australia
or ancient Europe somewhere, in a meadow,
forcing the gods to roar. They call it Uranic,
a heavenly force, sometimes almost a voice,
locked up in that whirling stone, dear father.

MARK RUDMAN
from Bottles

Misère: La seule chose qui nous console de nos misères est le diver-
tissement, et cependant c'est la plus grande de nos misères, car c'est
cela qui nous empêche principalement de songer a nous, et qui nous
fait perdre insensiblement.

—PASCAL

1

In Bellevue's "Emergency Ward," the diagnosis is not,
as was first thought, "a mild stroke,"
but "acute intoxication" of alcohol and a diabolical
mixture of seven tranquilizers, painkillers, and sleeping pills.
No wonder he couldn't speak. . .
and lay there on the floor beside the bed . . . .
I can't think of anything to say except
"you could have fallen and hit your head."

You might have fallen dead.

(He doesn't know I know the "diagnosis.")

"I don't know what happened to me," he says,
as his eyes scan the bureaus for bottles.
"It's a mystery."

2

I used to hurl the bottles
against the back of motel walls,
away from the hum of the generators
or throw them out of hotel windows,
windows so high above the earth I hardly heard
the crash, only the silent explosion of relief
when I knew the alcohol was gone from the room.
(I never thought of anybody being down below!)

My father never protested, never commented,
never acknowledged the emptiness, the empties,
would simply say, "Be right back,"
and return with the sack
in which the bottles clanged
hollowly like church bells.
"More ice, more ice," he would intone,
in case it should melt before morning.

My son, learning to stand, cocks
his forefinger at the dresser lamp
and utters something like *ite, ite.*

Ice: Gesturing at any clinking glass
he clutches it with both hands,
puts it to his lips and,

sucking and sighing,
tries to down the contents in one gulp,
tossing it back so fast he could choke, or soak,

reaches in, gobbles more ice,
and says *I, I,* through bulging cheeks
as it dissolves; then he coos.

3

I had a high school romance with the bottle too . . . .
And there I am entering the State Liquor Store
in Phoenix on a dark spring night
holding a borrowed I.D.
with the borrowed face
of a 23-year-old,

whose hair stands erect as a rooster's comb,
whose mouth is forced into a joyless grin,
whose eyes glaze over some inner pinwheel;
who looks as buzzed as Yves Tanguy
toward the end . . . ;
frightened, I stand outside,
16 years old, begging a stranger
to get me a bottle.

4

The thrill of it all.
Bottle bottle on the wall.
Ask it anything . . . .

The bottle talks.
Walks not so good.
The bottle knows

your unthought thoughts,
knows better
than you how

you feel about what;
it has plumbed
the unthinkable

alive and risen
filled with air.
Whatever you've repressed

the bottle will tell.
The bottle will tell
you anything unless

you ask,
specializes in spite,
knows by heart one

monologue which ends
with its premise . . . .
"Don't abandon me."

RITA DOVE
Taking in Wash

Papa called her Pearl when he came home
drunk, swaying as if the wind touched

only him. Towards winter his skin paled,
buckeye to ginger root, cold drawing
the yellow out. The Cherokee in him,
Mama said. Mama never changed:
when the dog crawled under the stove
and the back gate slammed, Mama hid
the laundry. Sheba barked as she barked
in snow or clover, a spoiled and ornery bitch.

She was Papa's girl,
black though she was. Once,
in winter, she walked through a dream
all the way down the stairs
to stop at the mirror, a beast
with stricken eyes
who screamed the house awake. Tonight

every light hums, the kitchen arctic
with sheets. Papa is making the hankies
sail. Her foot upon a silk
stitched rose, she waits
until he turns, his smile sliding all over.
Mama a tight dark fist.
Touch that child

and I'll cut you down
just like the cedar of Lebanon.

ALICIA OSTRIKER
The Leaf Pile

Now here is a typical children's story
that happens in gorgeous October
when the mothers are coming
in the afternoon, wearing brisk boots
and windy skirts to pick up
the little children from the day care center

Frost in the air
the maples golden and crimson
my son in a leaf pile in the playground dreaming
I am late, the playground is almost
empty, my husband will kill me

I gather my son to go home,
he forgets his sweater in the playground and I send him back
he dawdles, he is playing with leaves
in his mind, it is already a quarter
to six, will you come on I say

and hurry along the corridor, there are yellow and blue rocket
paintings, but I feel bad and ask what did you do today,
do you recognize this story, the way he stands and picks
his nose, move I say, do you want dinner or not
I'm going to make a nice dinner, fried chicken

I wheedle, so could you please walk a little
faster, okay, I walk a little faster and get upstairs
myself, pivot on boot-heel, nobody there,
he is putting something in his mouth, his sable eyelashes
downcast, and I am swooping down the stairwell screaming

> damn you
> that's filthy
> I told you not before dinner

We are climbing the stairs
and I am crying, my son is not crying
I have shaken him, I have pried the sweet from his cheek
I have slapped his cheek like a woman slapping a carpet
with all my strength

> mothers are very strong
> he is too young to do anything about this
> will not remember he remembers it

The mind is a leaf pile where you can bury
anything, pain, the image of a woman
who wears a necklace of skulls, a screaming woman
you dig quickly and deposit the pulpy thing
you drop leaves on it and it stays there, that is the story

that is sticking in my mind as we push
the exit door, and run through the evening wind
to my car where I jerk the gearshift and pick
up a little speed, going along
this neat suburban avenue full of maples
the mark of my hand a blush on my son's cheek.

TOI DERRICOTTE
Poem for My Father

You closed the door.
I was on the other side,
screaming.

It was black in your mind.
Blacker than burned-out fire.
Blacker than poison.

Outside everything looked the same.
You looked the same.
You walked in your body like a living man.
But you were not.

would you not speak to me for weeks
would you hang your coat in the closet without saying hello
would you find a shoe out of place and beat me
would you come home late
would i lose the key
would you find my glasses in the garbage
would you put me on your knee
would you read the bible to me in your smoking jacket after
        your mother died
would you come home drunk and snore
would you beat me on the legs
would you carry me up the stairs by my hair so that my feet
        never touch bottom
would you make everything worse
to make everything better

i believe in god, the father almighty,
the maker of heaven, the maker
of my heaven and my hell.

would you beat my mother
would you beat her till she cries like a rabbit
would you beat her in a corner of the kitchen
while i am in the bathroom trying to bury my head underwater
would you carry her to the bed
would you put cotton and alcohol on her swollen head
would you make love to her hair
would you caress her hair
would you rub her breasts with ben gay until she stinks
would you sleep in the other room in the bed next to me while
    she sleeps on the pull-out cot
would you come on the sheet while i am sleeping. later i look
    for the spot
would you go to embalming school with the last of my
    mother's money
would i see your picture in the book with all the other
    black boys you were the handsomest
would you make the dead look beautiful
would the men at the elks club
would the rich ladies at funerals
would the ugly drunk winos on the street
know ben
pretty ben
regular ben

would your father leave you when you were three with a mother
    who threw butcher knives at you
would he leave you with her screaming red hair
would he leave you to be smothered by a pillow she put
    over your head
would he send for you during the summer like a rich uncle
would you come in pretty corduroys until you were nine and
    never heard from him again

would you hate him
would you hate him every time you dragged hundred pound
    cartons of soap down the stairs into white ladies'
    basements

would you hate him for fucking the woman who gave birth
      to you
hate him flying by her house in the red truck
      so that the other father threw down his hat in the street
      and stomped on it angry like we never saw him
(bye bye
to the will of grandpa
bye bye to the family fortune
bye bye when he stomped that hat,
to the gold watch,
embalmer's palace,
grandbaby's college)
mother crying silently, making floating island
sending it up to the old man's ulcer
would grandmother's diamonds
close their heartsparks
in the corner of the closet
yellow like the eyes of cockroaches?

Old man whose sperm swims in my veins,

come back in love, come back in pain.

DIANE WAKOSKI
Wind Secrets

I like the wind
with its puffed cheeks and closed eyes.
Nice wind.
I like its gentle sounds
and fierce bites.
When I was little
I used to sit by the black, potbellied stove and stare
at a spot on the ceiling,
while the wind breathed and blew
outside.
"Nice wind,"
I murmured to myself.

I would ask mother when she kneeled to tie my shoes
what the wind said.

Mother knew.

And the wind whistled and roared outside
while the coals opened their eyes in anger
at me.
I would hear mother crying under the wind.
"Nice wind," I said,
But my heart leapt like a darting fish.
I remember the wind better than any sound.
It was the first thing I heard
with blazing ears,
a sound that didn't murmur and coo,
and the sounds wrapped round my head
and huffed open my eyes.
It was the first thing I heard
besides my father beating my mother.
The sounds slashed at my ears like scissors.
Nice wind.

The wind blows
while the glowing coals from the stove look at me
with angry eyes.
Nice wind.
Nice wind.
Oh, close your eyes.
There was nothing I could do.

TOI DERRICOTTE
My Father Still Sleeping After Surgery

In spite of himself,
my father loved me. In spite
of the hands that beat me, in spite
of the mouth that kept silent, in spite
of the face that turned cruel
as a gold Chinese king,
he could not control the love

that came out of him.
The body is monumental, a colossus
through which he breathes.
His hands crawl over his stomach
jerkily as sand crabs on five legs;
he makes a fist
like the fist of a newborn.

PAMALA KAROL [LA LOCA]
Crib Death

I.

My mother burned
tuna-and-peas casserole
while in a negligee
she made herself.
She hadn't put on her face,
just her lashes,
and her eyes looked
like something you'd see
in the refrigerator.
"God damn kids!!!" she'd scream
till her voile skin seemed
bolted with arteries.
A seraphic scarf
of organdy bloused
her hundred curlers.
*"God damn you! God damn
you all!"* She'd stand
there, practically naked
in the smoke,
with two gingham potholders
I'd made in my home
economics class.

II.

In the family room
my half-sister tittered
in her underpants
and nothing else.
Her father had his Brownie on
a tripod and a mammoth,
long moth-balled spot
accompliced him. Its spike,
the size of a soliloquy,
made the hot house hotter.
My sister batted camera-wise,
flat-chested in front
of the sewing machine
where her First Holy
Communion gown needed
sleeves. The good Mary
Janes stood by waiting
for the Savior.
I, under the table
with elbow grease,
watched my sister
buttering in tungsten.
Above, our mother
snipped and snipped
in acrimony of *"queers, queers
littering the world."*
Her cheap-chained silver
asteroid of Christ bucked
from breast to breast
as she bent to pink
the Battenburg
of my sister's veil.

III.

In the dark, "Gunsmoke"
and Miss Kitty's hips
careered off the Mad Magazines,
model cars and German Lugers
of the bedroom where

my older brother sat
masturbating. *"It's the glue,"*
lied the doctor of the candy-
apple rash that studded
my brother's hands. And even now,
a jalopy lay in sockets
on the boneyard of the Classifieds,
epoxy cooking in the plain
temperature of the television.
*"Look who thinks he's
an artist!"* our mother stabbed
when he brought home a pad
for practicing naked women.
While the flaming decals
and the six tailpipes set, he fleshed
with a blunt Ticonderoga.
Afterward, the bodies
crackled in a basket.
"Learn to draw!"
said the book of sulphur-
tipped, on its fly.

IV.

Smacked for thumb-sucking,
my baby brother lay
a formula of Bosco
shook with milk.
His lips could only touch
appliances. This was the crib
where he slaughtered his dolls.
A rayon brontosaurus,
an eyeless Fido, a kinky sloth
were his for smothering,
slamming on the head-
board, force-feeding
his pacifier.
On the badlands
of the shag, a child's .22
mustered with the raggedy
anns who got up every morning
to be shot at naptime.

At naptime my baby brother
dreamed of infancy:
Biting the heads off words,
teething on the consonants;
colicky in the bassinet
with its violent diaperpins.
He dreamed the first particles of sight,
the circumcision of the umbilicus,
the lungs electrocuted with air.
When he awoke, the nursery
was blue and motionless.

from The Mayan

Mine was the roistering brothel
where I was beaten at
age 8
for asking at the
dinner table
what the word *"fuck"* meant.
"Sex," she said,
"was meant to be learned in the gutter."

Brown as the arm of the
Mexican who tooled it
was the strap
with the thick nickel buckle
she carried on her shoulder
day and night
so that she could have me
anytime she wanted.
I ran and ran and
she would chase me
into cobwebs
and finally to the screen door
and it would have been so
easy to lift the latch
and run

But always,
the body that made my body
cut out my tongue.

One day
into the seraglio
came her new man.
She showed him my bound feet
and I called him
daddy.
Daddy was
as big as a door.

He wore green slacks and
a yellow shirt
with a plastic pen holder
in the shirt pocket
that said Drone Spark Plugs.
Soon, he had a belt too, which at
dinnertime hung over the back of his chair.
We were
a family.

*"When I'm through with you
you'll wish you were dead."*

And they would seize their routine
and I would lunge to the floor
the way I'd been taught
at Benjamin Franklin Elementary
when there was an air raid siren
the last Friday of every month
and you'd quickly hide under the table
with your knees and elbows tucked
into your body and your hands clasped
over your neck to protect your
cortex with your two little
seven-year-old hands
against the hydrogen bomb
when it dropped on you.
Although I had learned *"please"* and
"thank you" from Miss Mary on
Romper Room and how to make
paper ashtrays
there was never a coloring book
on pain.

"Kill her!"
my mother shouted with
each rotation of her arm
and my step-father would say
*"stop crying, I'm not going
to stop till you stop crying."*

I didn't know where to put my little make-believe
because I didn't have a
toy box or a cloak room.
So I searched for the gutter
where you are meant to learn things
and I went down,
down, deeper than you can know
below the world
where they keep the
lockers and the costumes
and I hid in the dark
and waited
until at shame I became a virtuoso.

They whipped till their arms
moaned
and then Onan the paterfamilias
would fall off me
with his belt lying sensitive
over his thigh
and my mother would take her seat
at the head of the table
chafed because she broke a fingernail.
I picked up their marriage
with both my hands
and I resumed my place
in the arrangement.

One inch taller than
my Patty McCoy doll
I asked,
as they taught me,
"May I be excused, please?"
It took me all night
to clear the table
and wash the dishes
and dream

that I had been adopted . . .
They sat in the living
room with cheap beers and
Bonanza.
I scrubbed the
pans till they shone
to prove we were puritans.
One night
the big white ranchers
were displaced
with Watts.
There was a refrigerator
on fire and people
running with pillows
and television sets.

I stood at the kitchen
door drying the broiler
and watched my mother and step-father
on the porch
screaming:
"Kill the niggers!"
I watched them. I watched them and watched them.
"Kill the niggers!"
my mother scorched
till she was dizzy
and the white dusk
blacked above her
and you got the feeling
of hell.
I watched them, hating together,
like a romance
singing for the annihilation
of human beings
with whoops and the swill of Coors.
This was how they remained
together
how he went to work
and came home
day after day
and made her car payments.

I went to bed.
He went to bed.

But she had her reasons
She had a migraine
insomnia
constipation
and the vapors.
All night long
my stepfather grew a beard
I dreamt about naked angels
and she lay
with the brothelry and hurly burly
of the Sylvania.
Why was I born?
Why was I born?
Why was I born?
Was all there was
that was hers.

TOI DERRICOTTE
Abuse

Mama, the janitor is kissing me. Don't tell me that, you
make me suffer. You always make me suffer. Mama, father
is beating me. Don't tell me that. What do you want me to
do? Mama, the janitor is coming in the house and wants to
feel me. Well, come here, come see the janitor and say
hello. I come in a starched pinafore and she stands at the
foot of the stairs as if she is proud. Where were you when
a man, a man who could fix a toy, stuck his tongue in my
mouth and rubbed his thing on my school uniform? When I
flew up the stairs into the arms of the Blessed Mother,
where were you? Wanting to bury your head in a tub of
warm water, heating dinner in your slip and socks with
half a can of flat beer. Where were you when he came with
his fists, after nights of "yes suh boss" and "no suh
boss," when he knocked us around and threw meat on the
table? Mama doesn't care. She puts her little hands in
the air and it still comes raining down. Everything's
neatly in place—every pin, every needle—but the walls are

coming apart. Roaches peek out of the cracks, their
feelers trembling; and the little girl is wiped across the
floor like a flour sack. She is decorated by love. Her
legs have stripes from beating. Later her father sponges
her eyes where tears spill like blood. She shuts down like
a factory—every thought, a hand without a way to work—or
lies in the dark like a whipped dog praying he'll come.

CHARLES WRIGHT

What I remember is fire, orange fire
from BLOODLINES

13

What I remember is fire, orange fire,
and his huge cock in hand,
Touching my tiny one; the smell
Of coal dust, the smell of heat,
Banked flames through the furnace door.

Of him I remember little, if anything:
Black, overalls splotched with soot,
His voice, *honey, O, honey* . . .
And then he came, his left hand
On my back, holding me close.

Nothing was said, of course—one
Terrible admonition, and that was all . . .
And if that hand, like loosed lumber, fell
From grace, and stayed there? We give,
And we take it back. We give again . . .

Note: The janitor, kindergarten; Corinth, Mississippi.

ELIZABETH McKIM
Taking the Name

> I cling to the edge
> of the saddle of terror
> my arms batter air

Pulled me into a bath/house and pushed me into a toilet
stall/ and pushed my head down/ and pulled my drawers
down/ and tried to ram it in from behind/like a sword/
like a billy club/he hurt me in my sex/and I gave up/ I
let him/ I was so scared/he had all the power/ and I had
none of the power/ and he came in where he didn't belong
and my body/ my good sexual laughing body grew cold and still
and dead/ and I held the small child in my arms/ and the moon
like a mother cried for her innocent child

> *hush now*
> *doncha cry*
> *momma loves you*
> *by and by*

And all the secrets/ floated away and melted/ and all the secrets
sang in the field of tears/ in the lake of pain/ sang and sang/
and went away again

My name was taken away/ my momma's name taken away/ the
goddess defiled in her own temple/ and all the women cried/ and
all the women cried/ and it was a shame/ a cryin' shame/ and
the world turned in on itself/ and stopped its breathing/
and from that time on/ everything was all wrapped up and covered
over/ and the child grew heavy and water/logged/ and couldn't
hold on/ no couldn't hold on/ no couldn't hold on/ to any thing
but her cryin' shame/ and her special sound/ her special sound

BRUCE WEIGL
The Impossible

Winter's last rain and a light I don't recognize
through the trees and I come back in my mind
to the man who made me suck his cock
when I was seven, in sunlight, between boxcars.
I thought I could leave him standing there
in the years, half smile on his lips,
small hands curled into small fists,
but after he finished, he held my hand in his
as if astonished, until the houses were visible
just beyond the railyard. He held my hand
but before that he slapped me hard on the face
when I would not open my mouth for him.

I do not want to say his whole hips
slammed into me, but they did, and a black wave
washed over my brain, changing me
so I could not move among my people in the old way.
On my way home I stopped in the churchyard
to try to find a way to stay alive.
In the branches a red-wing flitted, warning me.
In the rectory, Father prepared
the body and blood for mass
but God could not save me from a mouthful of cum.
That afternoon some lives turned away from the light.
He taught me how to move my tongue around.
In his hands he held my head like a lover.
Say it clearly and you make it beautiful, no matter what.

The Man Who Made Me Love Him

All I know about this man
is that he played the trumpet
from his bedroom window.
Evenings we could hear him
trying to play something

while we laughed at the din
and called him names.

I want to sing about this
but all I know
is that it was near dark
so I missed the way home
and stopped to rest in the churchyard
where gold carp lolled in the holy pond.

I was seven and the man who played the trumpet
took me to the roundhouse
where he said the hobos slept,
and though I knew the tracks
and the woods surrounding them,
I didn't know that secret.

He made me take him into my mouth,
my face rose and fell with his hips
and the sun cut through boxcars
waiting to be emptied.

II. VIOLENCE AND RACE

the face of poetry must be fire erupting volcanos,
hot silk forging new histories,
poetry delivering light greater than barricades of
silence . . .

—HAKI R. MADHUBUTI

from "Killing Memory"

JAMES WELCH
The Man From Washington

The end came easy for most of us.
Packed away in our crude beginnings
in some far corner of a flat world,
we didn't expect much more
than firewood and buffalo robes
to keep us warm. The man came down,
a slouching dwarf with rainwater eyes,
and spoke to us. He promised
that life would go on as usual,
that treaties would be signed, and everyone—
man, woman and child—would be inoculated
against a world in which we had no part,
a world of money, promise and disease.

from Blackfeet, Blood and Piegan Hunters

. . .
Comfortable we drink and string together stories
of white buffalo, medicine men who promised
and delivered horrible cures for hunger,
lovely tales of war and white men massacres.
Meaning gone, we dance for pennies now,
our feet jangling dust that hides the bones
of sainted Indians. Look away and we are gone.
Look back. Tracks are there, a little faint,
our song strong enough for headstrong hunters
who look ahead to one more kill.

Plea To Those Who Matter

You don't know I pretend my dumb.
My songs often wise, my bells could chase

the snow across these whistle-black plains.
Celebrate. The days are grim. Call your winds
to blast these bundled streets and patronize
my past of poverty and 4-day feasts.

Don't ignore me. I'll build my face a different
     way,
a way to make you know that I am no longer
proud, my name not strong enough to stand
     alone.
If I lie and say you took me for a friend,
patched together in my thin bones,
will you help me be cunning and noisy as the
     wind?

I have plans to burn my drum, move out
and civilize this hair. See my nose? I smash it
straight for you. These teeth? I scrub my teeth
away with stones. I know you help me now I
     matter.
And I—I come to you, head down, bleeding from
     my smile,
happy for the snow clean hands of you, my
     friends.

ADRIAN C. LOUIS
Sunset at Pine Ridge Agency

Waiting for you waiting for foodstamps,
I watch an old man with a brown face
and swollen red nose
lower the flag
at the Pine Ridge Agency
and try to control it
against the frivolity
of a slapping wind.

The Medusan stripes are phallic
and seem to ejaculate

the yellowed stars
into faded blue cloth.

Rouge smothers the sagging breasts
of these Indian hills
which hide the unmarked grave
of Crazy Horse.

In cubist shadows adjoining
the roseate patina
drunks stab and rape
(Is there a difference?)
other drunkards and nobody
gives a good God damn.

This Indian nation is in anarchy
dancing awkwardly toward the day
when it will fall off the edge
of the bed of the world
and awake to its own suicide.

Fullblood Girl on a Blue Horse

for Luis Rodriguez

I don't know
why I sobered up and moved
from the rez down the road
twenty miles to this cow town.
The rednecks across the street
are partying and I am trying
to mow my weedy lawn.
One cowpoke chucks a beer
bottle and it explodes
on the street bordering
the back edge of my yard.
This Nebraska town
(Population: 1,492)
is a dried-up cowturd.
The only thing that keeps
it from blowing away
is the money the Indians

bring to town and yet
the greatest redneck joy is
hating and baiting Indians
and trying to keep us down.

Another bottle shatters . . .
I want to go get my pistol
and make that heifer-humper
crawl up the street
and pick up the glass shards
with his teeth and tongue.
My blood pressure is rising.
I want to make him cry
and piss his pants, but
I simply shut off the old mower
and shuffle down to the Post Office.
Maybe their party will be done
by the time I get back.
Maybe Wovoka's dream will
finally come true and all
the white folks will vanish.
Might as well hope it will snow
in July or the Pope will do
a commercial for condoms
and dildos and such.

This mailbox outside the Post Office
on Main Street is my thought temple.
It stands alone in defiance
of nature and winos.
Like a fortress of solitude
or a holy shrine,
it's a steel blue altar
for scrawled secrets of mine.
Those sacred words
I place inside
are useless bits
of wounded pride
and more that matters
even less but today
something is amiss.
A beautiful girl straddles
the mailbox.

Definitely high on something
this long-legged fullblood
girl with teenaged thighs
sits astride the cold blue
box like it is a wild stallion flying
her over this prairie town and
stampeding my once-green heart.
She smiles at me when I open
the chute and slowly insert
my letters and bills.
Grandfather! For one brief
moment of pained delight
electricity snaps in my pants.
Then I turn and strut
proudly towards home
but halfway there
I feel old and tired
and I pray I don't shoot me
some rednecks today.

Pabst Blue Ribbon at Wounded Knee

Between the sensual
and the visionary
how can our spirits extinguished by spirits
discern the dancing of ghosts?
These black basin hills are tipped in blue
and our space is cracked
under blackest sky.
We wait and wonder and don't ask why
we sit in our cars drinking Pabst Blue Ribbon.
The snow is waiting in the air.
Snow geese are wailing in the air
as we slur our song of self-pity.
Beneath the church on the hill to our right
lies the blinding blight of our souls:
sanctified by the Christian cross
we are at no loss to understand
the one mass grave that America gave
to those eighty-four warriors
and their sixty-two women and kids.

JOY HARJO

For Anna Mae Pictou Aquash

For Anna Mae Pictou Aquash, Whose Spirit Is Present Here and in the Dappled Stars (for we remember the story and must tell it again so we may all live)

Beneath a sky blurred with mist and wind,

                                  I am amazed as I watch the violet

heads of crocuses erupt from the stiff earth

                             after dying for a season,

as I have watched my own dark head

                        appear each morning after entering

the next world

             to come back to this one,

                    amazed.

It is the way in the natural world to understand the place

                        the ghost dancers named

after the heart/breaking destruction.

                Anna Mae,

                    everything and nothing changes.

You are the shimmering young woman

                  who found her voice,

when you were warned to be silent, or have your body cut away

from you like an elegant weed.

          You are the one whose spirit is present in the dappled stars.

(They prance and lope like colored horses who stay with us

        through the streets of these steely cities. And I have seen them

        nuzzling the frozen bodies of tattered drunks

                       on the corner.)

This morning when the last star is dimming

                    and the buses grind toward

the middle of the city, I know it is ten years since they buried you

    the second time in Lakota, a language that could

            free you.

I heard about it in Oklahoma, or New Mexico,

      how the wind howled and pulled everything down

  in a righteous anger.

    (It was the women who told me) and we understood wordlessly

the ripe meaning of your murder.

    As I understand ten years later after the slow changing

        of the seasons

that we have just begun to touch

    the dazzling whirlwind of our anger,

we have just begun to perceive the amazed world the ghost dancers

  entered

    crazily, beautifully.

In February 1976, an unidentified body of a young woman was found on the Pine Ridge Reservation in South Dakota. The official autopsy attributed death to exposure. The FBI agent present at the autopsy ordered her hands severed and sent to Washington for fingerprinting. John Trudell rightly called this mutilation an act of war. Her unnamed body was buried. When Anna Mae Aquash, a young Micmac woman who was an active American Indian Movement member, was discovered missing by her friends and relatives, a second autopsy was demanded. It was then discovered she had been killed by a bullet fired at close range to the back of her head. Her killer or killers have yet to be identified.

LESLIE MARMON SILKO
The Fourth World

The old-time people always told us kids to be patient, to wait, and then finally, after a long time, what you wish to know will become clear. The Pueblos and their paleo-Indian ancestors have lived continuously in the Southwest of North America for twelve thousand years. So when the old-time people speak about "time," or "a long time," they're not speaking about a decade, or even a single lifetime; they can mean hundreds of years. And, as the elders point, out, the Europeans have hardly been on the continents of the Americas five hundred years. Still, they say, the longer Europeans or others live on these continents, the more they will become part of the Americas. The gravity of the continent under their feet begins this connection, which grows slowly in each generation. The process requires not hundreds but thousands of years.

The prophecies foretelling the arrival of the Europeans to the Americas also say that over this long time, all things European will eventually disappear. The prophecies do not say the European people themselves will disappear, only their customs. The old people say that this has already begun to happen, and that it is a spiritual process that no armies will be able to stop. So the old people laugh when they hear talk about the "desecration" of the Earth. Because humankind, they know, is nothing in comparison to the Earth. Blast it open, dig it up, or cook it with nuclear explosions: the Earth remains. Humans desecrate only themselves. The Earth is inviolate.

> Ts'its'tsi'nako, Thought-Woman,
> is sitting in her room
> and whatever she thinks about
> appears.

> She thought of her sisters,
> Nau'ts'ity'i and l'tcts'ity'i,
> and together they created the Universe
> this world
> and the four worlds below.

> Thought-Woman, the spider,
> named things and
> as she named them
> they appeared.

> She is sitting in her room
> thinking of a story now

> I'm telling you the story
> she is thinking.

So perhaps it did not seem extraordinary to the old people that a giant stone snake formation was found one morning in the spring of 1980 by two employees of the Jackpile uranium mine. The mine is located near Paguate, one of seven villages in the Laguna Pueblo Reservation in New Mexico. The employees, both Laguna Pueblo men, had been making a routine check of the mine when they discovered the biomorphic configuration near the base of mountainous piles of uranium tailings. The head of the snake was pointed west, its jaws open wide. The stone snake seemed to have always been there. The entire formation was more than 30 feet long and 12 inches high, an eccentric outcrop of yellow sandstone mottled and peppered with darker iron ores, like the stone that had once formed the mesas that had been swallowed up by the open-pit mine.

Reports of the snake formation were at first met with skepticism. The miners must be joking. People from Paguate village and other Laguna Pueblo people had hunted rabbits and herded sheep in that area for hundreds of years. Over time, wind and rain might uncover rock, but the process required years, not weeks. In any case, Laguna Pueblo people have a name and a story for every oddly shaped boulder within two hundred miles—no way could anything like this giant stone snake have escaped notice. The mine employees swore they had walked the same route twice each month for inspections and seen nothing, and then suddenly one morning the stone snake was there, uncoiling about 300 yards from a jackpile mine truckyard. And soon there was a great deal of excitement among Pueblo religious people because the old stories mention a giant snake who is a messenger from the Mother Creator.

> Ma'shra-True'-Ee is the giant serpent
> the sacred messenger spirit
> from the Fourth World below.
> He came to live at the Beautiful Lake, Ka-waik,
> that was once near Laguna Village.
> But neighbors got jealous.
> They came one night and broke open the lake
> so all the water was lost. The giant snake
> went away after that. He has never been seen
> since.
> That was the great misfortune for us, the
> Ka-waik'meh,
> at Old Laguna.

Before the days of the mining companies, the people of Paguate village had fields of corn and melons and beans scattered throughout the little flood plains below the yellow sandstone mesas southeast of the village. Apple and apricot orchards flourished there too. It was all dry farming in those days, dependent on prayers and ceremonies to call in the rainclouds. Back then, it was a different world, although ancient stories also recount terrible droughts and famines—times of great devastation. When large uranium deposits were discovered only a few miles southwest of Paguate village in the late '40s and early '50s, the Laguna Pueblo elders declared the Earth was the sacred mother of all living things, and blasting her wide open to reach deposits of uranium ore was an act almost beyond imagination. But the advent of the "cold war" had made the mining a matter of national security, and the ore deposits at the Jackpile mine were vast and rich. As wards of the federal government, the small Pueblo tribe could not prevent the mining of their land. Now, the orchards and fields of melons are gone. Nearly all the land to the east and south of Paguate village has been swallowed by the mine; its open pit gapes within two hundred yards of the village.

Before world uranium prices fell, the mining companies had proposed relocating the entire village to a new site a few miles away because the richest ore deposit lay directly under the old village. The Paguate people refused to trade their old houses for new all-electric ones; they were bound to refuse, because there is a small mossy spring that bubbles out of the base of a black lava formation on the west side of Paguate village. This spring is the Emergence Place, the entrance humans and animals used when they first climbed into this, the Fifth World. But the mining companies were not to be stopped; when they couldn't move the people, they simply sank shafts under the village.

When the mining began, the village elders and traditionalists maintained that none of their people should work at the mine and participate in the sacrilege. But the early 1950s were drought years, and the Laguna people, who had struggled to live off their fields and herds, found themselves in trouble. Moreover, World War II and the Korean War had ushered in other changes within the community itself. The men who returned from military service had seen the world outside. They had worked for wages in the army, and when they came home to Laguna they wanted jobs. Consequently, increasing numbers of Laguna men, and later women, began working the mine. Cranky old traditionalists predicted dire results from this desecration of the Earth, but they had never been very specific about the terrible consequences. Meanwhile Laguna Pueblo became one of the few reservations in the United States to enjoy nearly full employment. Twenty-five years

passed, and then something strange and very sad began to happen at
Paguate village.

"Tonight we'll see
if you really have magical power," they told him.

So that night
Pa'caya'nyi
came with his mountain lion.
He undressed
he painted his body
the whorls of flesh
the soles of his feet
the palms of his hands
the top of his head.

He wore feathers
on each side of his head.

He made an altar
with cactus spines
and purple locoweed flowers.
He lighted four cactus torches
at each corner.

He made the mountain lion lie
down in front and
then he was ready for his magic.

He struck the middle of the north wall.
He took a piece of flint and
he struck the middle of the north wall.
Water poured out of the wall
and flowed down
toward the south.
He said, "What does that look like?
Is that magic powers?"
He struck the middle of the west wall
and from the east wall
a bear came out.
"What do you call this?"
he said again.

"Yes, it looks like magic all right,"
Ma'see'wi said.
So it was finished
and Ma'see'wi and Ou'yu'ye'wi
and all the people were fooled by
the Ck'o'yo medicine man,
Pa'caya'nyi.

From that time on
they were
so busy
playing around with that
Ck'o'yo magic
they neglected the Mother Corn altar.

They thought they didn't have to worry
about anything.

Pueblo communal systems value cooperation and nonaggression above all else. All problems, including the most serious, are resolved through negotiation by the families or clans of the aggrieved parties. Perhaps the harshness of the high desert plateau with its freezing winters and fierce summer droughts has had something to do with the supreme value the old people place upon cooperation and conciliation. For where margin for error is slender—even during the wet years—a seemingly trivial feud might hinder the mobilization and organization necessary to protect crops threatened by dramatic conditions of nature. Moreover, this system of cooperation extends to all living things, even plants and insects, which Laguna Pueblo elders refer to as "sisters and brothers," because none can survive unless all survive.

Given this emphasis on balance and harmony, it was especially painful and confusing when, in 1973, Paguate became one of the first American communities to cope with the unexpected tragedy of a teenage suicide pact. The boys and girls all had attended Laguna-Acoma High School, and all but one of the suicides lived at Paguate. Some left suicide notes which made reference to an agreement the young people had made secretly. "Cherylyn did it Saturday so now it's my turn," for example, was the way one note read.

The Laguna people had already suffered suicides by army veterans sick with alcohol. But the suicide victims at Paguate had been the brightest and most promising students at the school. The usual psychological explanations—unstable family environment, absence of one parent, alienation—don't seem to apply here, as not one of the students had come from a poor or troubled family, and in fact most had grown up in the house inhabited by their families for hundreds of years and were surrounded by supportive groups of relatives. While teachers and families tried in vain to learn more about the suicide club, it eventually claimed several lives.

While suicide took its toll, the Pueblo community was disrupted by another horror, an apparently motiveless murder. A Saturday night party in Paguate turned into a slaughter. Two young men were hacked to death at the kitchen table by their friend, who had invited them to stop by the party after they got off swing-shift at the mine. The killer then bullied another friend to drive a car they "borrowed," and while the friend drove around the reservation, the killer randomly dumped body parts in the weeds along the way. The impulse to pick up the shiny new axe had been irresistible, the killer later said. He could not explain the murder of his two friends.

But the old people have their own explanation. According to the elders, destruction of any part of the Earth does immediate harm to all living things. Teachers at Indian School would ridicule these ideas; they would laugh and say "How stupid you Indians are! How can the death of one tree in the jungle possibly affect a person in New York City!" But isn't it far more obvious these days how important that single tree in the rain forest of Brazil really is to the Manhattanite? And in the same way, the mesas of sandstone seemingly devoured by the uranium mine are as important, as essential. If it has taken environmental catastrophe to reveal to us why we need the rain forest, perhaps we might spare ourselves some tragedy by listening to the message of sand and stone in the form of a giant snake. Perhaps comprehension need not come from obvious catastrophes—like the destruction of the ozone layer—but through more subtle indications like a stone snake come to remind us that violence in the Americas—against ourselves and against one another—can run as deep, but only as deep, as the deepest shafts with which humankind has pierced the Earth.

When I saw the stone snake in June of 1980, I could hear the clanking and creaking of giant earthmovers on the other side of the mounds of tailings. The Jackpile mine generators roared continuously night and day, seven days a week. At noon, when Jackpile did the blasting, everyone made sure to be indoors because potato-size rocks frequently landed on Paguate doorsteps. (These were the normal, day-to-day living conditions of the Laguna Pueblos in and around Paguate for many years.) Old barbed wire had been loosely strung along a few makeshift juniper posts until someone provided a sagging barrier of chain-link fencing, intended to protect the stone snake from livestock and photographers. Corn meal and pollen, bits of red coral and turquoise had been sprinkled over the snake's head as offerings of spirit food. Holy people from tribes as far away as Canada and Mexico had come to see the giant snake.

There have been attempts to confine the meaning of the snake to an "official" story suitable for general consumption. But the Laguna Pueblos go on producing their own rich and continuously developing body of oral and occasionally written stories that reject any decisive conclusion in favor of ever increasing possibilities. This production of multiple meaning is in keeping with Pueblo cosmology in general. For the old people, no one person or thing is better than another; hierarchies presuming superiority and inferiority are considered absurd. No thing or location on the Earth is of greater or lesser value than another. And this means that any location can potentially become a sacred spot.

Thus, outsiders who visit the American Southwest are often confused by the places in which they find sacred altars or sites of miraculous appearances of blessed virgins or others (could it be the notion of original sin that causes Europeans to define "the sacred" as the virginal or pure?). They expect to find the *milagro* of Nuestra Senora de Guadalupe in pristine forest grottoes, *not* on the window glass of a cinder-block school building in a Yaqui Indian town; of Jesus' face in a rainbow above Yosemite Falls, not on a poor New Mexican woman's breakfast tortilla. The traditional notion of the wondrous in a splendid setting befitting its claim is subverted here in this landscape where the wondrous can be anywhere and is everywhere. Even in the midst of a strip-mining operation.

Just as the Laguna prophecies say that all things European will eventually pass away, Europeans have, particularly in the last century, predicted the demise of all things Native American. In the late 1960s, anthropologists lugged their tape recorders to the Pueblos, so that they might have the elders record stories and songs that would be lost when they passed away. Most of the Laguna elders agreed to make the tape recordings, but a few of the old people took a hard line. They said that what is important to our children and our grandchildren will be remembered; what is forgotten is what is no longer meaningful. What is true will persist. In spite of everything, Ma^{oh'}shra-True'-Ee, the sacred messenger, will appear again and again. Nothing can stop that. Not even a uranium mine.

> The wind stirred the dust.
> The people were starving.
> "She's angry with us,"
> the people said.
> "Maybe because of that
> Ck'o'yo magic
> we were fooling with.
> We better send someone
> to ask our forgiveness."
>
> They noticed hummingbird
> was fat and shiny
> he has plenty to eat.
> They asked how come he
> looked so good.
>
> He said
> Down below
> Three worlds below this one
> everything is
> green
> all the plants are growing
> the flowers are blooming.
> I go down there
> and eat.

YUSEF KOMUNYAKAA
New Amsterdam

With dental picks & horsehair
      brushes, the archaeologists
            take us back slowly

to the Dutch West India Company
      on Manhattan Island. The ghost
            of each coffin outlines the soil . . .

Big Manuel, Little Anthony, Simon
      Congo, & all the others—everything's
            tallied & measured till a faint

picture begins to show through.
      Bones & teeth are recounted. DNA
            extracted. Coins are stolen

off the eyes of skeletons that face
      Judgment Day. They find copper
            shroud pins & buttons

from a British marine officer's uniform.
      So much has rotted into a mute
            incandescence we can't see.

The stone houses & gristmill
      come to life in New Amsterdam; just
            over there the Sheep Pasture

overlooks a Dutch Reformed Church.
      How did God get mixed up
            in slavery? Maybe this

was answered by William Kieft
      when he armed the slaves
            with hatchets & half-pikes

against Indian tomahawks.
      These yellow bones can tell Forensic
            more than they can reveal to us

about the blacks who were freed
        to fight Indians & raise wheat,
                beans, corn, & peas. If

Pedro Negretto spoke, would he
        only talk about his hogs?
            Their souls haunt

the top floors of skyscrapers.
        Now, as the shiny tools sing
            among shards of pottery

& bone, progress has stopped
        one hundred feet in the air.
           Navajo steelworkers

are eclipsed like silhouettes against
        the Manhattan sky as we
           try to remove spells

& pray the bones will tell us
        how much pressure it takes
           to shape a diamond.

HENRY JOHNSON
The Middle Passage

Twelve years old,
naked and shivering
on the main deck, her eyes
wide-open, their pupils
bottomless and black
because a huge red haired
sailor pins her shoulders
to the deck, her ankles
clasped by two seamen,
cursing the smell
of her small black body.
Why does this surface

from some book I no longer
can name, as clear
as the three-masted ship
on its cover? I remember
checking the book
out of the library,
in the spring, and
as I brought it home
my mother was fleeing
through the streets of Brooklyn,
her screams like
chalk scraping the blackboard
at school, where the maps
of the world were pinned
to the blackboards like
my father laid out
across the hood of a white Plymouth,
held down by six white men
red faced drunk, tight fists
rising and falling and rising
until a surge of life
propelled him from the hood
wielding his huge fists.
There must have been crewmen
whose lust shriveled
in the moonlight,
but it is the man
with the glorious red hair
at the helm, and muscles writhing
as he laughs,
booming across the waves
bumping and scraping
against the side
of the ship, feet
dangling above
the foaming water
like my father's feet
above the sidewalk
as he wrestled
on the hood of the car
beneath those clubs of flesh and bone
beating like distant drums
as the man with the red hair

fashions a harness
around Leana,
her slim body descending,
plunging as the rope plays out.
I see the long dark shape
slashing toward her, she
is pulled forward, and
out of the sea, the shark
breaking foam, glistening
slickly in the moonlight,
a touch, a heavy splash,
a scream. Her left leg
ended at the knee,
and still they took her
to the deck, again
her body stump beating
like my mother's heart and
my father's heels
beating against the fender
of the car, against the planking
and against the man
who was not a man breaking
into the history of a child princess
who woke one night
to a world of moonlight
and spreading fires,
and now, too weak to scream,
lies somewhere on a ship
in the middle of my life.

RITA DOVE
Someone's Blood

I stood at 6 a.m. on the wharf,
thinking: *This is Independence, Missouri.*
I am to stay here. The boat goes on to New Orleans.
My life seemed minutes old, and here it was ending.

I was silent, although she clasped me
and asked forgiveness for giving me life.

As the sun broke the water into a thousand needles
tipped with the blood from someone's finger,

the boat came gently apart from the wharf.
I watched till her face could not distinguish itself
from that shadow floated on broken sunlight.
I stood there. I could not help her. I forgive.

YUSEF KOMUNYAKAA
Modern Medea

Apex, triangle . . . a dead child
On the floor between his mother, Margaret,
& four slavecatchers in that Cincinnati
Hideout. Blood colors her hands

& the shadow on the wall
Is a lover from the grave.
She sacrificed her favorite
First. He must've understood,

Stopped like a stone figure.
Where's the merciful weapon, sharp
As an icepick or hook knife?
We know it was quick,

A stab of light. Treed,
As if by dogs around an oak.
She stands listening to a river
Sing, beggin salt for her wounds.

History Lessons

1.

Squinting up at leafy sunlight, I stepped back
& shaded my eyes, but couldn't see what she pointed to.
The courthouse lawn where the lone poplar stood

Was almost smooth as a pool table. Twenty-five
Years earlier it had been a stage for half the town:
Cain & poor white trash. A picnic on saint augustine
Grass. A few guitars & voices from hell.
No, I couldn't see the piece of blonde rope.
I stepped closer to her, to where we were almost
In each other's arms, & then saw the flayed
Tassel of wind-whipped hemp knotted around a limb
Like a hank of hair, a weather-whitened bloom
In hungry light. That was where they prodded him
Up into the flatbed of a pickup.

2.

We had coffee & chicory with lots of milk,
Hoecakes, bacon, & gooseberry jam. She told me
How a white woman in The Terrace
Said that she shot a man who tried to rape her,
How their car lights crawled sage fields
Midnight to daybreak, how a young black boxer
Was running & punching the air at sunrise,
How they tarred & feathered him & dragged the corpse
Behind a Model T through the Mill Quarters,
How they dumped the prizefighter on his mother's doorstep,
How two days later three boys
Found a white man dead under the trestle
In blackface, with the woman's bullet
In his chest, his head on a clump of sedge.

3.

When I stepped out on the back porch
The pick-up man from Bogalusa Dry Cleaners
Leaned against his van, with an armload
Of her Sunday dresses, telling her
Emmitt Till had begged for it
With his damn wolf whistle.
She was looking at the lye-scoured floor,
White as his face. The hot words
Swarmed out of my mouth like African bees
& my fists were cocked,

Hammers in the air. He popped
The clutch when he turned the corner,
As she pulled me into her arms
& whispered, *Son, you ain't gonna live long.*

MICHAEL WARR
We Are All the Black Boy

In his mouth
An icy steel,
Notched barrel in his mouth
Fingered by a sadist
With an omnipotent badge,
Disgusted by the boy's blackness
'fraid of the rebelliousness
In his predator walk,
In his street corner
Disposition,
In his Niggers With An Attitude
"fuck tha police" lyrics.
For this audacity
Hands behind the back
And bullet in the head
His former breathing valuable
Only to the ghetto undertaker
With the one permanent job.
They are wise to fear.
Our blood
Cannot be retracted
Without redemption.

Cabrini Gulag

North of the congestion
Of Bavarian status symbols
On Division's most dreaded blocks
A concrete gulag confines

Regenerated slaves.
Their overseers
Visible but not obvious,
With Wang computers
Supplanting leather whips.
Their offspring running manuevers
In a warzone called playground.
Upstairs in open cubicles
Mothers worry of another
Policeman's mistake.

About the tenant's ankles
Retarding momentum toward escape
Hangs memory of the first
Shackled family
Scattered on forced arrival.
Cutting into the tenant's wrists
A string of prime male specimens
Bartered in down-the-river trade.
Beneath emblazoned Troop jackets
The brand of chattel slavery
Still rises like black belt mountaintops
Above surrounding skin.
Not a scar just psychological,
But as material as roaches,
Street corners and billy clubs.
A wound reopened systematically,
Inflicted with economic anarchy
And "No Help Wanted" signs.

WILLIAM LOGAN
Seductions of the Swimming Club

The working mothers never worked aloud,
those afternoons spent poolside, lean and tanned
amid the apparitions of the crowd.
The petals of their suits were caked with sand.
No black face ever troubled their repose.
At sunset servants in white uniforms

showered the greasy dust off with a hose
as summer broke the dark with lightning storms.
We drank in their politeness like a sin;
each deferential sir, each honeyed ma'am
reminded us that powers ranged above us.
Our mothers drank martinis and sweet gin:
we were too young for anyone to love us.
That fall our boys invaded Vietnam.

ETHERIDGE KNIGHT

A Fable

for Etheridge Bombata and Mary Tandiwe

Once upon a today and yesterday and nevermore there were 7 men and women all locked / up in prison cells. Now these 7 men and women were innocent of any crimes; they were in prison because their skins were black. Day after day, the prisoners paced their cells, pining for their freedom. And the non-black jailers would laugh at the prisoners and beat them with sticks and throw their food on the floor. Finally, prisoner #1 said, "I will educate myself and emulate the non-colored people. That is the way to freedom— c'mon, you guys, and follow me." "Hell, no," said prisoner #2. "The *only* way to get free is to pray to my god and he will deliver you like he delivered Daniel from the lion's den, so unite and follow me." "Bullshit," said prisoner #3. "The *only* way / out is thru this tunnel i've been quietly digging, so c'mon, and follow me," "Uh- un," said prisoner #4, "that's too risky. The only right / way is to follow all the rules and don't make the non-colored people angry, so c'mon brothers and sisters and unite behind me." "Fuck you!" said prisoner #5. "The *only* way / out is to shoot our way out, if all of you get / together behind me." "No," said prisoner #6, "all of you are incorrect; you have not analyzed the political situation by my scientific method and historical meemeejeebee. All we have to do is wait long enough and the bars will bend from their own inner rot. That is the *only* way." "All of you are crazy," cried prisoner #7. "I'll get out by myself, by ratting on the rest of you to the non- colored people. That is the way, that is the *only* way!" "No-no," they / all cried, "come and follow me. I have the / way, the only way to freedom." And so they argued, and to this day they are still arguing; and to this day they are still in their prison cells, their stomachs / trembling with fear.

HAKI R. MADHUBUTI
Aberrations

hair, color and quiet desperation in the last quarter of the
20th century.

post-1986 and it is still political to, consciously or unconsciously,
desire hair that is straight or curly in the fashion of europe
and to seek the lightest and "fairest" of people to love while
proclaiming one's deepest and undying commitment to all that is
black, and on paper, beautiful.

the utter pain of being dark
and women,
living among men who despise
the "nappiness" of head & the
hue of skin sunbaked before birth.

the unimaginable hurt of being dark
and short and man,
living among images of vikings
tall and conquering
"angel-like" roaming the earth
seeding the wombs of the vanquished coloreds.

the war was fought
when being natural became anti-self & unkind,
the war was confusing
when we lied to ourselves to convince
the nonbelief in us,
the war was in disorder
when practice became embarrassing,
the war was lost
when self-hatred emerged as a force greater than the
scorn of sworn enemies.

beauty and being beautiful is not the question.
all people desire beauty.
a full people needs love,
music and flowers in their lives.

whose love remands the answer?
whose music determines the call?
whose beauty decides the winner?
whose culture dictates the dance?

what is the color and texture of your flower?

TOI DERRICOTTE

A Note on My Son's Face

I.

Tonight, I look, thunderstruck
at the gold head of my grandchild.
Almost asleep, he buries his feet
between my thighs;
his little straw eyes
close in the near dark.
I smell the warmth of his raw
slightly foul breath, the new death
waiting to rot inside him.
Our breaths equalize our heartbeats;
every muscle of the chest uncoils,
the arm bones loosen in the nest
of nerves. I think the peace
of walking through the house,
pointing to the name of this, the name of that,
an educator of a new man.

Mother. Grandmother. Wise
Snake-woman who will show the way;
Spider-woman whose black tentacles
hold him precious. Or will tear off his head,
her teeth over the little husband,
the small fist clotted in the trust at her breast.

This morning, looking at the face of his father,
I remembered how, an infant, his face was too dark,

nose too broad, mouth too wide.
I did not look in that mirror
and see the face that could save me
from my own darkness.
Did he, looking in my eye, see
what I turned from:
my own grandmother
bending over gladioli in the field,
her shaking black hand defenseless
at the shining cock of flower?

I wanted that face to die,
to be reborn in the face of a white child.
I wanted the soul to stay the same,
for I loved to death,
to damnation and God-death,
the soul that broke out of me.
But when I peeked in the basket,
I saw the face of a black man.

Did I bend over his nose
and straighten in with my fingers
like a vine growing the wrong way?
Did he feel my hand in malice?

Generations we prayed and fucked
for this light child,
the shining god of the second coming;
we bow down in shame
and carry the children of the past
in our wallets, begging forgiveness.

II.

A picture in a book,
a lynching.
The bland faces of men who watch
a Christ go up in flames, smiling,
as if he were a hooked
fish, a felled antelope, some
wild thing tied to boards and burned.
His charred body

gives off light—a halo
burns out of him.
His face is scorched featureless;
the hair matted to the scalp
like feathers.
One man stands with his hand on his hip,
another with his arm
slung over the shoulder of a friend,
as if this moment were large enough
to hold affection.

III.

How can we make
from a dream
we are born into,
that shines around us,
the terrible bright air?

Having awakened,
having seen our own bloody hands,
how can we ask forgiveness,
bring before our children the real
monster of their nightmares?

The worst is true.
Everything you did not want to know.

The Weakness

That time my grandmother dragged me
through the perfume aisles at Saks, she held me up
by my arm, hissing, "Stand up,"
through clenched teeth, her eyes
bright as a dog's
cornered in the light.
She said it over and over,
as if she were Jesus,
and I were dead. She had been
solid as a tree,

a fur around her neck, a
light-skinned matron whose car was parked, who walked on swirling
marble and passed through
brass openings—in 1945.
There was not even a black
elevator operator at Saks.
The saleswoman had brought velvet
leggings to lace me in, and cooed,
as if in the service of all grandmothers.
My grandmother had smiled, but not
hungrily, not like my mother
who hated them, but wanted to please,
and they had smiled back, as if
they were wearing wooden collars.
When my legs gave out, my grandmother
dragged me up and held me like God
holds saints by the
roots of the hair. I begged her
to believe I couldn't help it. Stumbling,
her face white
with heat, she pushed me through the crowd, rushing
away from those eyes
that saw through
her clothes, under
her skin, all the way down
to the transparent
genes confessing.

At An Artists Colony

BLACK ARMS

A group of us are sitting around the TV room. Ray, a painter from
the South, is talking about how hard his mother works. He says: "I told
her all you need is a pair of good black arms." The others snicker.

I am new here. All I want to do is get along. I say nothing, though
now I know there is a part of me that is a joke to this man—my
washerwoman great grandmother, my cook grandmother.

I will be silent. I want him to like me. I want to tell him how he
hurts me. I want to speak. But then the colonists will say: "You know

how sensitive they are." I will be labeled. And for six weeks, the only black person, I will never be able to sit at the dinner table without "Black Arms."

DINNER TIME

Last night at the dinner table, John, a man who didn't know I'm black, noticed the book of women's diary writing which has a section of *The Black Notebooks* in it.

He asked me to see the book and when he took it, I could see he wasn't going to just skim over the table of contents. He went directly for my story, putting down his fork, and began to read. I felt a coldness, like a breeze ruffling a curtain on a line. The other dinner tables were quiet; many of the colonists don't know I'm black. I could just hear him blurt loudly, "I didn't know you're black. You don't look black. How did you get that color?"

I don't like to lose control of my identity that way. I fear being the center of attention, like an animal in a cage prodded and poked by onlookers.

The man, fortunately, kept his comments to the quality of the work. "This is great. It sent a shiver up my spine, It's dramatic."

The other people at the table didn't know the content. Not that I mind every person at the colony knowing I'm black. I don't care, and I am proud of my work. But when several come at me from all sides, I don't know which way to turn. Heaven help me if I should show anger or be defensive.

John wouldn't let it alone. Later, as several of us were sitting around the fireplace, he said, "You should read this article in *The Times.* You'll like it. It reminds me of your book." I hadn't seen the article, but I knew it must be about black people. As soon as he knew I was black, I became a category, and anything he reads by or about a black person reminds him of me.

A Chinese man who has also read my book said, "This article is nothing like the writing in Toi's book," I was glad he spoke, defending the uniqueness of my experience.

Later, John was playing pool. I was sitting twenty feet away and noticed him staring at me. I thought he was thinking I was attractive and was beginning to feel flattered. Suddenly he yelled across the room, "You should really read that article. You'll find it interesting. It's really timely."

Another man in the room called: "What's the article about?"

"Racism," he yelled back.

The people in the room looked up. I felt the conversation go out of my hands.

The other man said, "That isn't timely. It's ongoing and eternal."

I was glad somebody spoke and it wasn't me.

THE TESTIMONY OF INNOCENCE

Last night I went over to Marty's studio to share my work. She read some of my diary entries and I read some of her poems. She said she felt my diary entries were extremely important. She asked me who they were addressed to, and I read her the diary entry which described my audience: all the people in my past, black and white, who represent the internalized process of racism within me.

In 1976, when I began writing *The Black Notebooks*, I wrote mainly to myself, although at the back of mind was an idea that maybe someday, I would get the courage to make it public. The idea was to tell the truth as deeply as I could, however painful, but also to write for the larger human community. I know that sounds ridiculously grandiose, but I felt an honest confession would have merit. My negative self-concept made me trust myself to be more egoless than some writers whose descriptions of racism seem to be testimonies of their own innocence—and I have always distrusted that, both from whites and blacks.

My skin color causes certain problems continuously, problems which open the issue of racism over and over, like a wound, a chronic wound—a stigmata. These openings are occasions for re-examination. My skin color keeps things, literally, from being either black or white.

My decision to make more of my entries public comes from my meeting at the colony with a political activist, Pat, who, when I showed her my most scary black hatred entries, still loved me, showed me the mirror of acceptance. How I loved her for that!

I'll publish. I'll make a name for myself; I'll make money. I'll win the love of my relatives and get a professorship at a university. I'll win a movie contract and play the heroine of my own story. It seems awful to hope success will come out of such disaster.

Not to worry, Pat says, writing about racism doesn't make you successful, it makes you ignored.

RAY

Yesterday, after breakfast, I saw him lumbering toward his jeep. He looked a little lost; several of his close friends have left the colony. I had heard him say another gem this morning, "I wish I had ten little black women to sew the holes in that canvas . . ."

Every time the opportunity comes to talk to him the time doesn't seem right. Either other people are around or there's another problem. After his art show last night, I stayed longer than anyone, but he seemed depressed with people's reactions. It would have been piling shit on top of shit if I had tried to talk to him; and I don't think he would have heard what I was saying. I found myself listening to his worries, reassuring him, and kicking myself for being a coward.

But this morning was perfect. I know he often goes into town for donuts. I had been on my way to my studio, but I turned in my tracks.

Sitting in the donut shop, I waited for a relaxed moment. The comforting cups of coffee were placed before us. He lit a cigarette. "There's something I have to tell you," I said. "I'm black, and last week when you made the comment about black arms, it made me feel bad. And this morning you said something else about little black women sewing holes in the canvas." I didn't say it in a mean voice, just a human voice, one on one. (Inside, I'm saying, Why can't I just blurt it out? Why do I have to be so careful?)

I tried not to look at his face so I could get my words out, but I caught a glimpse and saw a muscle twitching in his cheek, his mouth was slightly open, and he was listening to me intently. I went on, "You see, I wanted to say something to you when this happened last week, but I didn't want to say something that would make people look at me as if I'm different. Sometimes when people find out I'm black, they treat me differently from then on. So when people say things that hurt me, I don't know what to do. I want to tell them. But, at the same time, I'm afraid I'll be hurt even more if I do."

He started to explain. "When I said that about 'black arms,' I was repeating something my mother-in-law said, and I was repeating it because I was horrified by it. What you feel must be similar to what I feel at my wife's house, because I am the only goy." I was happy that he was identifying with me, but I didn't want him to spend fifteen minutes explaining his life. I just wanted to tell him my pain and make sure he got my message. "Please, I don't want to put you on the spot. I just want you to understand my feelings. Do you understand? What do you hear me saying?" He said, "I hear you saying that certain comments which other people make without sensitivity have great poignancy to you because you are black." That wasn't exactly what I was saying, but it seemed close. Besides, it had taken all the bravery I could muster to come this far, I couldn't press him further.

In the past, I have left conversations like this empty, not getting what I wanted. I thought it was rage I wanted to vent. But yesterday, because he listened, because I had waited for the right moment and asked for what I wanted, I thought, maybe I've found the answer. From now on, if I just wait, if I just talk about my feelings honestly, if I don't expect the person to say something to take my pain away, if I just ask him or her to repeat back what I said until they've understood, then everything will be fine.

I want so much to find a formula! Of course, there is none. Sometimes it will come out O.K., like yesterday, and sometimes I will walk away with a hole in my heart that all the little black women in the world cannot sew up.

SATURDAY NIGHT

Several colonists sat around trying to have fun on a Saturday night. We miss New York, movies, Chinese restaurants. We talked about feminism, about how, these days, many of the young girls have babies while in high school.

A Southern lady said, "That's what black girls have been doing for years. They have babies and their families raise them. Maybe it's catching up with white girls." This is the same woman who three days ago was talking about how black people have "funny" names. "They name their kids the strangest things." I thought about the twins in New Jersey whose mother had honored the doctor who had delivered them by giving them names he suggested: Syphily and Gonorra.

This woman loves to talk about black people. She's our resident expert. She said, "There aren't any black people here. I haven't seen any."

"Yes there are," I said, smiling.

"Who?"

"You're looking at one."

"You're not really black. Just an eighth or something."

"I don't know how black I am, but I am black."

"Was your mother black?"

"My mother, my father, my grandparents. They are black, and they look just like me."

"How do you know you're black?"

"I'm black because black people were the first people I touched and loved."

A woman at the table said, ""Did you read the article in *The New York Times* that said if they were strict about genetics, sixty percent of the people in the United States would be classified as black?"

I looked about the table. I was laughing. The others were not. They were worried about how black I was and they should be worrying about how black *they* are.

I thought of all the little white children, the light of their mothers' and fathers' eyes, in Montana, in flat Wyoming, in Idaho, in lake-filled Michigan; I thought of that "funny" blackness inside of them, a kernel in each little heart put there, somehow in the night, like a visit from the tooth fairy.

I thought of the layers of lies of the first generation which covered that mystery up, the layers of repressed questions in the second generation which decomposed into layers of unconsciousness. Layer after layer, till one day little children walk around with unconsciousness laid over their minds like shrouds, pretty little children in pinafores with a nigger maid who has a funny name. Somewhere babies are popping out of women and no one understands where they come from.

I smile at the little heart of darkness in sixty out of a hundred babies. The drop of blood that can't lie to statistics, that will be bled out, measured, and put in a crystal tube.

That blood gives those little ones a special light. Wherever I look I see brothers, sisters, who want to break out of their cramped skins, singing with love.

THAT

Marty said yesterday she was surprised that Pat had called the colony a "white establishment," and said she was uncomfortable with some of the people. Marty hadn't noticed any of "that." Had I noticed any of "that?"

I was on guard. So many times if a black person admits discomfort, the white person then says that the black person must be "sensitive — paranoid"—not responding to the present environment, which is safe and friendly, but responding to something in the past. They want to hear that the white people in this environment (themselves) are fine. It's the black person who is crazy.

I said, "It is not something that is done consciously; but most of the white people here have had limited exposure to blacks; there are bound to be great problems in communication. There are some people who hate and fear blacks and don't want to be under the same roof. For example, Jan told me that Sandra said, when she saw no black people in the dining room, 'Good. I'm glad there are no black people. After New York, this is refreshing.'"

Marty said sometimes when she is with black people, she doesn't know what to do; no matter what she does it seems to be the wrong thing.

She told me how she had invited a black woman, a lawyer, over to her house for dinner and during the dinner conversation, the guests at the table started talking about Arabs raising the price of everything in England. Marty said she didn't think they were saying anything racist, and even if they were what did the Arabs have to do with this black woman? But the woman stood up from the table and said "I'm sorry, I find this conversation extremely embarrassing." Marty asked me did I think the woman was right to do that?

I told her, "Marty, frequently white people who have been made uncomfortable by something a black person says or does, go to another black person to try to ease the pain, to feel vindicated. First of all, I wasn't there, so I don't know what she responded to. Secondly, there would be no way to find out unless both of you could sit down and really talk to each other."

Marty said, "That will never happen because she has never asked me out, and when I called her she was cold."

I said, "Black people don't like pain either."

I thought of how sad it is—how a black person and a white person are not just two individuals who have to decide whether they like each other, but representatives carrying huge expectations, stereotypes they must scale like dangerous mountains trying to reach each other.

JAN'S STUDIO

I visited Jan yesterday. I went there feeling greatly honored that she had asked me, since most artists prize their time alone and don't want to be disturbed. I had just come into her room, sat down on the mattress, received a cup of tea, when she took off Mozart and asked me if I wanted to hear one of her favorite records, a record about Attica. The hair on the back of my neck stood up. What connection had she made between me and Attica?

Give her a chance, I thought, calming myself, maybe it's just a coincidence.

It was atrocious. A white band had taken the departing words of a prisoner and repeated them over and over as if we were certain to catch the significance. Atonal music played in the background; everything got louder and crashed to an end.

I sat there feeling the need to receive her gift with enthusiasm. She waited. The only word that came to my mind was "interesting."

After she took the record off, she started flipping through her collection of classical music to find something else especially for me. "I have a record by Paul Robeson. Would you like to hear that?" Oh God, I thought, it wasn't a coincidence. Give up hope you who enter.

"No thank you."

She seemed puzzled and at a loss. Finally, she asked, "There is a picture around here of a black man I liked. I slept with him. Would you like to see that?"

I gaped at her innocent face: Jan, the woman whom I head toward at dinner time because she is not pompous or intimidating, one of the only people here I feel comfortable with.

I told her that just because I am black doesn't mean I am one-dimensional. I am interested in many things, just as she is. I like classical music and know quite a bit about it. She said, "But my other black friends like it when I play those records." She looked genuinely hurt.

I told her all black people are different. She said, "But I've tried so hard. I'm tired of always trying to please them." She looked at me in anger. I was one more proof of her inadequacy. I should have taken whatever was offered and let her feel generous and good.

I left abruptly, sorry for my anger, sorry for what I had learned about her, sorry that she had lost her feeling of closeness, however illusory, to black people—sorry, sorry, sorry—and somehow to blame. I had felt close to her, now I distrusted my instincts, and dreaded a deeper isolation here than ever before.

JAZZ

Now that I am the "known" black here, everything with a tinge of blackness on it is delivered to me.

Mark, the composer, who has been talking about Mozart at the dinner table for days, comes running up to me this afternoon when he sees me on the path, his face lit like a beacon. He doesn't even bother with a greeting.

"Guess what I've been doing today?" he blurts out.

I can't imagine.

"I've been writing JAZZ," he presents, as if it is a Cartier jewel on a silver platter.

What am I supposed to say? You must be a really nice white guy? Thanks for taking us seriously?

"Good for you," I answer, and walk on as quickly as possible.

CRAZY THOUGHTS

How beautiful the view from my desk of wild flowers through the cathedral-tall window. I watch the lovely black birds. How kind the lunch on my doorstep, the vegetable torte with white cream sauce, the chocolate cake. How pleasing the flower on the table, the yellow Victorian sofa, the barn of colorful chickens. Kind and specific the words in the office, the locks on my doors. I am treated like a queen. But when the lights go off, I face my fears.

Why is my stomach in knots? Why do I fear that during the night I'll be smothered? I think poison gas will come out of the register. I think the people are monsters, not artists, and during the night they will implant a small radio in my brain. How can I think this? Memory of my father being smothered by a pillow my grandmother put over his head when he was three? In the morning I am ashamed.

I try desperately to make friends, hoping I will actually feel that trust that makes the knots in my stomach loosen. I was terrified to come here; I always feel frightened, except when I'm near home. I trust no one—especially not myself.

I try to do my work. This is a perfect environment. No cleaning. No cooking. I needn't even go to get my lunch; it is placed in a basket outside my door by a man on tiptoes. Wood is stacked. I make a fire. I sit in the sun. I want to be grateful. I am grateful. But the sickness of fear backs up in my throat like phlegm.

In the kitchen the cook speaks softly. I want to sit by her all day and stay away from the roads on which I have been hurt by a word. But she is cooking and I don't want to bother her.

Please, let me not bother anyone or anything. Let me leave the tub without a hair. Let me not speak to those who turn their bodies slightly away from me. I must not notice this.

No one can help. Only *I* myself. But how can I let go? My face is a mask, like Uncle Tom's, my heart twisted in rage and fear.

AFTER

After I came back I was sick for several weeks. I felt completely wrung out, run down. I had left smiling, beaming, thanking everyone; the kitchen help, the office help, the yard help, everyone for their kindness. My friend came to pick me up. The night before we were to drive home, I sat with her in the restaurant—the first black face I had seen in weeks—and, for an instant, I felt my body falling under me, as if I had slipped under the wheels of a train. I had almost made it until the last minute, keeping a stiff upper lip, and here I was, so close to the end, finally about to lose it.

They were so sorry to see me go they offered me a stay of two more weeks. If I stayed I would prove my desperate bravery to myself. But I declined. I was tired of feeling frightened and wanted to go home where I felt safe.

A Jewish activist friend returned from the colony shortly after and asked me to please write a letter telling them how hard it was to be the only black person there. She had found the same token black during her stay. I postponed it and postponed it. I didn't want to do it. I had been a success—I had gone some place far from home and stayed four weeks without having a nervous breakdown. And they had tried to do everything to please me—cook, clean after me, put wood in my fireplace. I didn't have the heart to tell them I had been miserable and frightened all the time. Besides, I wanted to be a "successful" black person, a person whom they would ask back, a person who would ease the way for other blacks. "See, we're not as bad as you thought."

The day my friend returned from the colony she was full of news about how she had written a letter to the board, sent names and addresses of black artists. The president had talked to her for a half hour about how pleased he was with her efforts. The next day she called me, despondent. Her editor had called her from her large publishing house—they were remaindering her last book. I felt so sorry for her. I told my husband about her efforts at the colony, and how she had come home to this big disappointment. "I'm not surprised," he said. "Somebody from the colony must have gotten to somebody at her publishing house and iced her." I looked at my husband angrily. "Oh, that's silly, I said. One has nothing to do with the other." But I felt the ground under me sinking.

NIKKI GIOVANNI

To Be Black in America
is to constantly be at war

19 October 1990

Violence, Rap Brown was fond of saying, "is as American as apple pie." Rap, being his usual succinct self, was right. But does that make "violence" right? Probably if I were contemplating "violence" twenty years ago I would not reach the conclusions I do today. I'm not crazy enough to think that the violence of the oppressed is the same as the violence of the oppressor and I do charge the oppressor with stopping the violence; yet, violence is not a good idea. If there is one real conclusion I have reached in forty-seven years it is that the ends and the means are indistinguishable. I don't think I would take back anything I wrote; I certainly don't apologize for anything I've thought but if human growth is to be meaningful I cannot do violence to my own heart and mind by pretending that nothing has changed.

To be Black in America is to constantly be at war, I believe; with yourself, with your dreams, with the people with whom we live. When you leave your domicile in the morning, and sometimes even when you stay there all day, there is the ever present fear of assault whether physical or mental. There is something about, well, life that makes you nervous. In many respects the violence of some whites is the easiest to take because it is physical and immediate. It hurts but if you survive you can categorize it, and therefore dismiss it, by saying "white folks." The violence, both physical and mental, that Blacks do to ourselves is more difficult. That violence takes away safety. The violence of child abuse, wife beating, drug taking is much harder to codify because somehow we victims feel we have brought this on ourselves. The violence of rape by a stranger is much more mentally acceptable than the violence of rape by Uncle Bubba, if you follow me. Certainly it is still rape but now the safety of home has been violated. Having lived in New York City for eleven years I got used to being mugged; I moved when my apartment was broken into. Am I saying I prefer a white collar criminal? You bet. I was still robbed but we didn't have to communicate and negotiate about it.

We need to study white Americans. There have been massive studies about Blacks trying to understand our situation. Yet, in all fairness to us, we did not make this situation. It's all but pointless to say we were brought here against our wills three hundred years ago because clearly we are not going anywhere else. Yet is it not we who keep the racial wars hot. We keep responding to what white America is doing to us. Louis Lomax, the journalist, wrote a book about the Black Muslims: *The Hate That Hate Produced.* We cannot fairly charge the victim with changing the atmosphere yet, since I am of the victim group, I know we are the ones upon whom change is incumbent. I have very little faith that white American will rise to the challenge. In other words, Martin Luther King and Malcolm X were right. You need to believe that your enemy would like to do the right thing while you need some muscle to get his attention.

I have been watching the "animal rights" people with interest. They find it perfectly acceptable to murder a dean at The University of Tennessee because he used animals in his research, but they walk over the homeless in their leather shoes. I watch anti-smokers feel perfectly justified in cursing the smokers never once trying to equate the automobile they drive with the pollution they ingest. Hatred, in other words, is serious business. King was just a bit more right than Malcolm because King did not want Black Americans to become what we were fighting against. I have seen enough of all sides to know the coin is round and rolls when pushed.

It's easy enough to say stop the hatred and that will stop the violence, but I don't think so. Or maybe stop the violence and that will stop the hatred, and yet something is still missing. Mostly we are responsible for our own acts. That's clear and simple. We can become the fools we see or we can change. There is no justification for Bensonhurst or the wilding in Central Park. The color of the victims cannot mitigate. It is wrong. When do we, our society, stop justifying violence? When is it as wrong to beat your wife, who, actually does not belong to you, as it is to beat a stranger as it is to beat your dog as it is to bomb a plane as it is to run over a possum in the road? Am I looking for Utopia? Why not? Reality isn't so hot. Nobody said life would be easy. And, speaking of reality, nobody's life is. One of the hardest concepts to get across to humans is that our very existence, for the most part, is the end result of another action.

We cannot live with this nervousness. We cannot continue with this greed. We are being suffocated with this hatred and made crazy with this violence. Aldous Huxley said "Time must have a stop." I agree. The only promise by life is life . . . and nobody can say how long or how well. This is a small planet in a finite universe. We must close Pandora's box or we will close this universe of the yellow sun down. Mentally, I can handle it. Sampson is one of my personal heroes. Job is another. There are no compromises. Somewhere, somehow, we must cease to do violence to ourselves and each other. Or we, quite frankly, must cease.

PAMALA KAROL [LA LOCA]
Why I Choose Black Men For My Lovers

Acid today
is trendy entertainment
but in 1967

Eating it was eucharistic
        and made us fully visionary

My girlfriend and I used to get cranked up
        and we'd land in
        The Haight
        and oh yeah
        The Black Guys Knew Who We Were
        But the white boys
        were stupid

I started out in San Fernando
        My unmarried mother did not abort me
        because Tijuana was unaffordable
        They stuffed me in a crib of invisibility
        I was bottle-fed germicides and aspirin
        My nannies were cathode tubes
        I reached adolescence, anyway
        Thanks to Bandini and sprinklers

In 1967 I stepped through a windowpane
        and I got real
        I saw Mother Earth and Big Brother
        and
        I clipped my roots which choked in the
                concrete
                of Sunset Boulevard
        to go with my girlfriend
        from Berkeley to San Francisco
        hitchhiking
        and we discovered
        that Spades were groovy
        and
        White boys were mass-produced and
        watered their lawns
                artificially with long green hoses in
                West L.A.

There I was, in Avalon Ballroom
        in vintage pink satin, buckskin and
                patchouli,
                pioneering the sexual
                revolution

I used to be the satyr's moll, half-woman,
and the pink satin hung
            loose about me
            like an intention

I ate lysergic for breakfast, lunch and
                  dinner
            I was a dead-end in the off-limits of
                  The Establishment
                  and morality was open to interpretation

In my neighborhood, if you fucked around, you were a whore

But I was an émigrée, now
            I watched the planeloads of white boys fly
                  up from Hamilton High
            They were the vanguard
                  of the Revolution
            They stepped off the plane
                  in threadbare work shirts
                  with rolled-up sleeves
                  and a Shell Oil, a Bankamericard,
                  a Mastercharge in their back pocket
                  with their father's name on it
            Planeloads of Revolutionaries
            For matins, they quoted Marcuse and Huey Newton
            For vespers, they instructed young girls from
                  San Fernando to
                  Fuck Everybody
            To not comply, was fascist
I watched the planeloads of white boys
            fly up from Hamilton High

All the boys from my high school were shipped to
            Vietnam
And I was in Berkeley, screwing little white boys
            who were remonstrating for peace
            In bed, the pusillanimous hands of war protestors
                  taught me Marxist philosophy:
            Our neighborhoods are a life sentence
            This was their balling stage and they
                  were politicians
            I was an apparition with orifices

I knew they were insurance salesmen in their
    hearts
And they would all die of attacks
I went down on them anyway, because I had
    consciousness
Verified by my intake of acid
I was no peasant!
I went down on little white boys and
they filled my head with
    Communism
They informed me that poor people didn't have
    money and were oppressed
Some people were Black and Chicano
Some women even had illegitimate children
Meanwhile, my thighs were bloodthirsty
    whelps
and could never get enough of anything
and those little communists were stingy
I was seventeen
    and wanted to see the world
    My flowering was chemical
    I cut my teeth on promiscuity and medicine
    I stepped through more windowpanes
        and it really got oracular

In 1968
One night
The shaman laid some holy shit on me and wow
I knew
in 1985
    The world would still be white, germicidally
        white
    That the ethos of affluence
    was an indelible
    white boy trait
    like blue eyes
    That Volkswagons would be traded in for
        Ferraris
        and would be driven with the same
        snotty pluck that sniveled around
        the doors of Filmore, looking cool
I knew those guys, I knew them when they had posters of
    Che Guevara over their bed

They all had posters of Che Guevara over
        their bed
And I looked in Che's black eyes all
        night while I lay in those beds,
        ignored
Now these guys have names on doors on the 18th floor of
    towers in Encino
They have ex-wives and dope connections.
Even my girlfriend married a condo-owner in Van Nuys.

In proper white Marxist theoretician nomenclature, I was
    a tramp.
The rich girls were called "liberated."

I was a female from San Fernando
        and the San Francisco Black Men and I
        had a lot in common
        Eyes, for example
        dilated
        with the opacity of "fuck you"
        I saw them and they saw me
        We didn't need an ophthalmologist to get it on
        We laid each other on a foundation of
            visibility
        and our fuck
        was no hypothesis

Now that I was worldly
    I wanted to correct
    the nervous blue eyes who flew up from
    Brentwood
    to see Hendrix
    but
    when I stared into them
    They always lost focus
    and got lighter and lighter
    and
    No wonder Malcolm called them Devils.

MARTÍN ESPADA
Niggerlips

Niggerlips was the high school name
for me.
So called by Douglas
the car mechanic, with green tattoos
on each forearm,
and the choir of round pink faces
that grinned deliciously
from the back row of classrooms,
droned over by teachers
checking attendance too slowly.

Douglas would brag
about cruising his car
near sidewalks of black children
to point an unloaded gun,
to scare niggers
like crows off a tree,
he'd say.

My great-grandfather Luis
was un negrito too,
a shoemaker in the coffee hills
of Puerto Rico, 1900.
The family called him a secret
and kept no photograph.
My father remembers
the childhood white powder
that failed to bleach
his stubborn copper skin,
and the family says
he is still a fly in milk.

LUIS J. RODRIGUEZ
'Race' Politics

My brother and I
—shopping for *la jefita*—
decided to get the "good food"
over on the other side
        of the tracks.

We dared each other.
Laughed a little.
Thought about it.
Said, what's the big deal.
Thought about that.
Decided we were men,
not boys.
Decided we should go wherever
we damn wanted to.

Oh, my brother—now he was bad.
Tough dude. Afraid of nothing.
I was afraid of him.

So there we go,
climbing over
the iron and wood ties,
over discarded sofas
        and bent-up market carts,
over a weed-and-dirt road,
into a place called South Gate
—all white. All American.

We entered the forbidden
narrow line of hate,
imposed,
transposed,
supposed,
a line of power/powerlessness
full of meaning,
meaning nothing—
those lines that crisscross

the abdomen of this land,
that strangle you
in your days, in your nights.
When you dream.

There we were, two Mexicans,
six and nine—from Watts no less.
Oh, this was plenty reason
to hate us.

Plenty reason to run up behind us.
Five teenagers on bikes.
Plenty reason to knock
the groceries out from our arms—
        a splattering heap of soup
        cans, bread and candy.

Plenty reason to hold me down
on the hot asphalt; melted gum
        and chips of broken
        beer bottle on my lips
        and cheek.

Plenty reason to get my brother
by the throat, taking turns
        punching him in the face,
        cutting his lower lip,
        punching, him vomiting.
Punching until swollen and dark blue
he slid from their grasp
like a rotten banana from its peeling.

When they had enough, they threw us back,
dirty and lacerated;
back to Watts, its towers shiny
across the orange-red sky.

My brother then forced me
to promise not to tell anybody
how he cried.
He forced me to swear to God,
to Jesus Christ, to our long-dead
Indian Grandmother—
keepers of our meddling souls.

MARTÍN ESPADA

Cross Plains, Wisconsin

Blue bandanna
across the forehead,
beard bristling
like a straw broom,
sleeveless T-shirt
of the Puerto Rican flag
with Puerto Rico stamped
across the chest,
a foreign name on the license,
evidence enough
for the cop to announce
that the choice is cash or jail,
that today
the fine for speeding
is exactly
sixty-seven dollars,
and his car
will follow my car
out of town

From an Island You Cannot Name

Thirty years ago,
your linen-gowned father stood
in the dayroom of the VA hospital,
grabbing at the plastic
identification bracelet
marked Negro,
shouting "I'm not!
Take it off!
I'm Other!"

The army photograph
pinned to your mirror
says he was,
black, Negro
dark as West Indian rum.

And this morning,
daughter of a man
from an island you cannot name,
you gasp tears
trying to explain
that you're Other,
that you're not.

JIMMY SANTIAGO BACA
The Handsome World

The handsome, broad-shouldered world, with
its great blue eyes, its thrashing and vigorous veins, its
rough hands fit for anything, turning, and its legs blocking
up the sky, giant world I live in, your tremendous embrace,
your uncombed hair during the workday, or at night, you
stand erect and glittering, escorting the most beautiful
women, and under the lights, I stand wondering if you are
a god, if other gods in their starry thrones lean forward
from their sleepy edens, to ponder on your growing arms,
your fuller voice, your looking up to them, and in your
eyes, a slight spark of renegade war, cries and shines
defiantly.

It's all well, husky barrel-chested cities
of America. Drowning in your liquor and gambling and clothes,
your rebels and libraries, your blood vessels filled and gorged
as if dams broke loose and hurtled toward gutters and gulches,
none can stop you, all rush to their boats made of bone,
and sails made of red cloth from the heart, and sail you to America,
waving to others, all passing, passing and floating by.
So in all your grand wonder and greatness,
I wonder, who am I here? And thinking of this, I feel like
driftwood, knocked and banked on any shore, grabbed by any
hand up high, carrying its weight, and I beneath, bubbling
for life, for each breath.
Then I said, I will prove I am someone.
I dropped what I was doing, and left with nothing but me.
Well, now, this is all I am, breathing with firm eye toward

the distance. Ah, how lovely, how happy I am to be just me.
I raise my pink gums like a wild chimpanzee, tilt my head back,
chortling white-toothed, at this amazing zoo and its visitors,
pockets filled with popcorn, and crunching candy apples,
I just laugh and jump down the road . . . walking all day, free
of my leash.

So this is who I am? The world a playground
of steel bars and merry-go-rounds? But you see the sun up
there? You see the sky, and how it drips with rain like old
rafters, and from its corners birds swoop out and dive, you
see this land, the uniformity against cruel angry mountains,
I see it all; the glare of chrome and glaze of windows,
the suspense and ambition of young boys playing baseball
in parks, and sidewalks splattered with the night's blood,

and the policemen sleeping with his wife and farting in
the bathroom, and then after, so groomed and polished,
passing shops along the street, hello he says to one,
hello to another. I sleep in the grass thinking of this,
and can be arrested for sleeping on the grass, and I laugh
looking at the sky, filling the sky with my laughter,
the treetops bend and birds scatter out.
I stand up, grass all around me, and start
walking through the tall grass, listening to myself live,
hearing my foot lift and set, carrying me
like a stray animal, a holy one who rose out of mud, with mind
of man, heart of earth, taking my body-form as others,
from now on, I scream and howl and love and laugh, I am me.

MARTÍN ESPADA
Nando Meets Papo

Somerset County, Maryland, August 1983

Nando was the one
from Legal Aid
who wore red suspenders
that spelled out
WORKER down one side

and SOLIDARITY
down the other,
biting like a watchdog
on a thin cigar,
with wild hair
and the dented-can grin
that made the landowners
in Somerset County
all sputter when he said
hola or hello.

He wasn't afraid of Papo either,
the cannonball-bellied crewleader
at Angelica
migrant labor camp.
even though Papo fired Shorty
for organizing,
then showed the chambers of his revolver
around camp,
boasting that any farmhand
who left the grounds
for the union or church
or to piss
could go al cielo
and tug at the robes of Jesus
that same day.

Tonque de queda: Curfew in Lawrence

Lawrence, Massachusetts, August 1984

Now the archbishop comes to Lawrence
to say a Spanish mass.
But the congregation understands
without translation:
the hammering of the shoe factory,
sweating fever of infected August,
housing project's asylum chatter,
dice on the sidewalk,
saints at the window,
two days' murky pollution of riot-smoke,
the mayor's denials.

Tonque de queda: curfew signs
outlaw the conspiracy of foreign voices
at night.
Barricades surround the buildings
window-black from burning, collapsed in shock.
After the explosion of shotgun pellets
and shattered windshields,
sullen quiet stands watching on Tower Hill,
trash, brick and bottle fragments
where the arrested kneeled, hands clapped
to the neck, and bodies with Spanish names
slammed into squad cars, then disappeared.

The mobs are gone: white adolescents
who chanted USA and flung stones
at the scattering of astonished immigrants,
ruddy faces slowing the car to shout spick
and wave beer cans.

Now the archbishop comes to Lawrence
to say a Spanish mass.
at the housing project where they are kept,
they're collecting money for bail.

LUIS J. RODRIGUEZ
Overtown 1984

Overtown—you are the last shred of America
        left in America.
You are the last ones to remain mute
        in the face of destruction.
You are the long evening descended
        into daybreak.
From the sockets of burning skulls
        come screams of retribution,
For our sons, for our daughters,
        for fathers forced into not being fathers,
        for mothers who only see the world
        through the tunnel of a child's long wail.

When you awoke again in flames,
        you carried me with you;
You, a face of fire, sweat across furrowed
        foreheads.
You, the bones of a dark time,
        of a stumbling down dilapidated steps.
It seemed an act of desperation, you alone
        against the Miami skies.
Alone in the shadow of palm trees.
Alone against the blackened batons
        of police power.
Alone against the newspapers & TV stations &
        suited officials at bus stops &
        politicians in marbled corridors
        who dared to call you "criminals."
Newspapers carried pictures of Overtown residents
        in paddy wagons, looking tired,
        forlorned.
Alone? Not really. Your long night took me in.

I watched the burning from outside my hotel
        room following the acquittal of a police
        officer who killed an unarmed Overtown boy.
Walking toward you, I was met by helmeted
        officers. By whirling lights and road blocks.
        I kept coming.
Near some apartments a boy started a fire.
Its flames were the brothers of Watts, Detroit,
        the Hough and Harlem.
Near a place of murder along a cement path,
        life came to life.
Under the streetlamps, under freeway passes
        and green palms, the darkness became
        glowy and red.

JOSÉ MONTOYA
The Uniform of the Day

Strong and bold,
they came — alone, in teams,
    droves — early on
to sociologize us an' to
    weaken us.

One day
there they wuz — in the barrio
    studying th' points, us —
y nosotros estudiando el punto
    scrutinizing as well
this army of scholars wearing
    corduroy and clip-boards
    and audacity huffing and puffing
    crooked briar pipes
an ours of deer horn, stone
or clay and wood, even —
good pipes, good smoke I miss,
    and I miss th' girls
    that loved boys, women
    men, and went on
    some even to graduate school.

. . . and my colega that has become
invisible on campus that I miss
from old action days now I see
on Saturday mornings strolling
there lonely in th' uniform.
    Corduroy jacket with elbow patches
    clutching a pipe, brow
    furrowed deep, suffering —
    yet, digging his latest
    findings, enjoying his
    cocker spaniel.

. . . why is that sound so succulent?
Spaniel — Spaniard — Hispanic, Hispaniel?
    Well, every uniform should have
    a dog — I myself walk the Derelict Dog

An 'en there's my own trapos —
my uniform de la calle — boogies
(baggies) khakis o gabardine o
sharkskins, gauchos en el
summer, workshirts for th' cold —
blue, cotton or Pendleton
and if colder my blue Sir Guy jacket,
calcos del fil
or Rockport bisquits
for diabetic feet y mi tapa
Stetson Beaver stingy brim
or watch cap!

    Now if that ain't a uniform!

And how absurd that
uniform must look on
Campus!

    As out of place as
    corduroy and briar
    pipes in th' Barrio

. . . but that's what the contract
called for, muy conformes
    in uniform.

Hispanic Nightlife at Luna's Cafe When th' Mexicans Came to Visit th' Chicanos in Califas

It is a well known fact
that in the education we got
from the Chicano movement
we discovered, affirmed
confirmed and reaffirmed
our "Indianness".

No sooner had our indigenismo
emerged fuerte y sano

from healing enjuagadas
cleansing and re-cleansing y mas
que fue reviviendo la
consencia Europea — that same
conquista attitude que
habiamos mandado a la madre
con Cortez y los Malinchistas
pero la mera madre nos/los
rechazo!

So today the struggle within
our Mejicanidad es una
lucha antigua entre lo Indio
y lo Europeo — and from
there the struggle/joda
vacillates entre Chicano/Hispano
Mejicano/Indio y hasta Latino
eres tu, bruto!
Quo Vadis, Chicano?
Me Pregunta un cuate firme
de Tepito.

Y le digo al Chilango de
la capirucha, que that's what
the Chicano needs to know
in Tewa or Apache
o hasta Azteca — a dilemma?
Tu dile, ma!

So the lines are drawn
and its not an Apache
or even an imperious Aztec
or a Tewa or two against
some Moor in Spain from Africa
or a Visigoth from up North.
It is about those of us
who are neither from
Mayan splendor nor Iberian
Gypsy-We who didn't
make it whole but almost,
casi-were not ni Moros
ni Negros, ni Blancos,
somos mas, Casi!

So the Casis, then, are
the ones on the line —
Casindios on one side
Casispanos on the other
los Casindios in their struggle
siguen al Masindio Masiso
y su Masisa de maiz
and the Casispano also
pronounced Cathispano by
the guey, venerate
al Machine y la Machine
sin rin ni matachin!

Solo casi nos queda
due nos libre
san Tin Tan
en calo
Ho!

A Chicano Veterano's War Journal

The A. P. photo on the front page
of the violence during the
elections en El Salvador
stuns all the sensibilities!

Chingao, carnal!

Ah-ummm-silence screams
in the mind! Four for four
and the circle around it!

Sad to think that todays
Chicanitos and the youth in general
have only that photo to measure
the carnage of war violence —
fueled by — who gives
a damn!

Whether it is greed
or ignorance, it
diminishes us!

And what about those
of us who already
served gallantly — blindly?

Who have in our own
Americanization witnessed
horror scenes too
similar in Vietnam
in Korea — in World War II.
Nosotros, los veteranos,
us! Cabrones!
Where are we?
To tell the youth
the horrible truth
to that A. P. photo —
about out barriadas,
Raza? The violence is here!

El Salvador is our
Barrio, Raza!
And how rapidly we
are letting our barrios become
the violence of future
A. P. war journalism.

PEDRO PIETRI
Beware of Signs

Beware of signs that say
"Aqui Se Habla Espanol"
Dollar Down Dollar A Week
until your dying days

BUEYNOS DIASS
COMO ESTA YOUSTED?
AQUI SAY FIA
MUEBLAYRIA
Y TELEVECION SETS
ROPAS BARRATOS
TRAJES Y ZAPATOS

PARA SUSHIJOS
AND YOUR MARIDOS
NUMAYROSAS COSA
PARA LA ESPOSA
KAY TIENAY TODO
KAY BUEYNO CREDITO
PUEDAY COMPRAR
MACHINAS DAY LAVAR
VACUM CLEANEROS
YOUSTED NAME IT
AND IF NOSOTROS
NO LO TENAYMOS
WE LOS INVENTAYMOS
IMMEDIATAMENTAY
JESS WE WILL
NADAQUIESIMPOSI
BLAYBLABLUDAGHAZ
OOLADUYAJAYEAHAZ
SI NO SAY NECESITA
NINGUNO DINEROS
SOLAMENTAY YOU SIGN
AQUI ON THIS LINE
Y TODO WILL BE FINE
MUCHAS GRACIAS SENOR
MUCHAS GRACIAS SENORA
AND DON'T FORGET
TO VUELVAY AGAIN
TELL ALL YOUR NEXT
DOOR VEYCINOS THAT
WITH EVERY TEN DOLLAR
PURCHASE THEY MAKE
LEY DEMOS UNO DISCO
DEY LA CANCION
DEY SU FAVORITO
TELEVICION PROGRAMA
simpleymentay maria
simpleymentay maria
maria maria ETCETRA
HASTA LA VISTO AMIGO

Beware of signs that say
"Aqui Se Habla Espanol"
Do not go near those places

of smiling faces that do not smile
and bill collectors who are well train
to forget how to habla espanol
when you fall back on those weekly payments

Beware! Be Wise! Do not patronize
Garbage is all they are selling you
Here today gone tomorrow merchandise

You wonder where your bedroom set went
after you make the third payment

Those bastards should be sued
for false advertisement
What they talk no es espanol
What they talk if alotta BULLSHIT

CARLOS CUMPIÁN
Veterano

Insect victories
fought over scum-cracked
concrete and colors
no one wants to see,
especially families in the park
as it gets dark, and the boys
make their runs for wine, reefer,
glue or some friendly doctor's pills.

Buzzed six to a car,
roaring past stoplights
so "Lil Juanito" can score
before there's no more
angel dust or 'cane
Tonight he got burned,
they might as well have sent
a drunk baboon on the deal.
"Pinche menso, why didn't you
check it?"

"Calláte tu hocico buey,
come caca
si no te gusta."
"Speak English cabron!"
"OK, con safos chicabacho."

It's swell-chest time and your pandilla
has got it bad, the magic markers are
almost empty and there's no more
white shoe shine.
The cross-town clubs, even the putos
from down the block, have painted
out your folk's marks.
So & so and so & so runs it,
there's hand signs and murder mouthing
and a fight for the crown,
when one of Beto's buddies lets you
know who runs it,
a fast blast from a stolen gun
then his slow life sentence.

Y tu en el mundo de mierda
piensas que eres muy cool
todos los chavos can't wait
to water down their lives for you,
pero you're always worried 'bout
who's watching your back
and if you'll hear the hammer go
click . . .

Didn't make it in school?
Trabajo ruins all your fun?
Change all that, get in with
the real gang-bangers' delight,
the original ruff-tuff-stuff,
join up con ese locos in the Marines.
Those guys have got everything!
Camouflage and M-16's,
they've kicked ass from the sangron
"Halls of Moctezuma" to the
terrorist resorts of Tripoli.

So get mad, make revenge your cohort,
be "bad" and live with the ganga

of your pitiful choice,
even if your deepest friend—
your inner voice, tells you
to do otherwise.
Listen here, bato con el mota brain,
listen and you'll catch the
click—as its owner yells,
"Yanquí!"

MARTÍN ESPADA

Tony Went to the Bodega
but He Didn't Buy Anything

para Angel Guadalupe

Tony's father left the family
and the Long Island city projects,
leaving a mongrel-skinny puertorriqueño boy
nine years old
who had to find work.

Makengo the Cuban
let him work at the bodega.
In grocery aisles
he learned the steps of the dry-mop mambo,
banging the cash register
like piano percussion
in the spotlight of Machito's orchestra,
polite with the abuelas who bought on credit,
practicing the grin on customers
he'd seen Makengo grin
with his bad yellow teeth.

Tony left the projects too,
with a scholarship for law school.
But he cursed the cold primavera
in Boston;
the cooking of his neighbors
left no smell in the hallway,
and no one spoke Spanish

(not even the radio).

So Tony walked without a map
through the city,
a landscape of hostile condominiums
and the darkness of white faces,
sidewalk-searcher lost
till he discovered the projects.

Tony went to the bodega
but he didn't buy anything:
he sat by the doorway satisfied
to watch la gente (people
island-brown as him)
crowd in and out,
hablando espanol,
thought: this is beautiful,
and grinned
his bodega grin.

This is a rice and beans
success story:
today Tony lives on Tremont Street,
above the bodega.

JANICE MIRIKITANI
Recipe

Round Eyes

Ingredients: scissors, Scotch magic transparent tape,
                eyeliner—water based, black.
                Optional: false eyelashes.

Cleanse face thoroughly.

For best results, powder entire face, including eyelids.
        (lighter shades suited to total effect desired)

With scissors, cut magic tape 1/16" wide, 3/4"-1/2" long—
depending on length of eyelid.

Stick firmly onto mid-upper eyelid area
        (looking down into handmirror facilitates finding
        adequate surface)

If using false eyelashes, affix first on lid, folding any
excess lid over the base of eyelash with glue.

Paint black eyeliner on tape and entire lid.

Do not cry.

Doreen

Doreen had a round face.
She tried to change it.
Everybody made fun
of her in school.

Her eyes so narrow
they asked if she could see,
called her moonface and
slits.

Doreen frost tipped her hair
ratted it five inches high,
painted her eyes round,
glittering blue shadow up to her brow.

Made her look sad
even when she smiled.

She cut gym all the time
because the white powder on her neck
and face would streak
when she sweat.

But Doreen had boobs
more than most of us Japanese girls

so she wore tight sweaters
and low cut dresses
even in winter.

She didn't hang
with us,
since she put so much time
into changing her face.

White boys
would snicker when she passed by
and word got around
that Doreen
went all the way,
smoked and drank beer.

She told us
she met a veteran
fresh back from Korea.

Fresh back
his legs
still puckered pink
from landmines.

She told us
it was a kick
to listen to his stories
about how they'd torture
the gooks
hang them from trees
by their feet
grenades
in their crotch
and watch
them sweat.

I asked her
why she didn't dig brothers.

And her eyes
would disappear
laughing

so loud
she couldn't hear herself.

One day,
Doreen riding fast
with her friend
went through the windshield
and tore off
her skin
from scalp to chin.

And we were sad.

Because
no one could remember
Doreen's face.

DWIGHT OKITA

The Nice Thing About Counting Stars

for Yoshio and Takeyo

In 1942, over 100,000 Americans of Japanese descent were evacuated from their homes
by the American government and forced to relocate in internment camps. They wound
up staying for three years. My mother, Patsy Takeyo Okita, was one of them. This poem
includes excerpts from her memoirs.

> "In the hot summers of the 30's, we would
> sit on the steps and sing for hours. We
> even counted the stars in the sky and it
> was always beautiful."

So my mother begins
writing her life down, Jackie Onassis
thinking in the car behind dark glasses.
She recalls the luxury
of growing up—she and her sisters
buying jelly bismarcks on Sundays
and eating them in the back seat
of their father's Packard

parked on the drive.
Pretending they were going
somewhere, and they were.
Not knowing years later they would
be headed for just such an exotic place.
Somewhere far from Fresno, their white stone house
on F Street, the blackboard in the kitchen
where they learned math,
                    long division, remainders,
        what is left
        after you divide something.

"When Executive Order 9066 came telling
all Japanese-Americans to leave their
houses, we cleared out of Fresno real
fast. They gave us three days. I remember
carrying a washboard to the camp. I don't
know how it got in my hands. Someone must
have told me—Here, take this."

They were given three days to move
what had taken them years to acquire—
sewing machines, refrigerators, pianos, expensive fishing
rods from Italy. A war was on—Japs
had bombed Pearl Harbor.
Burma Shave billboards littered the highways:

        SLAP

                    THE JAP

"Take only what you can carry."
My mother's family left the Packard
and with it left Sundays in the back seat.
Others walked away from acres of land,
drugstores, photo albums.

I think of turtles.
How they carry their whole lives
on their backs. My neighbor Jimmy
told me one night how they
make turtle soup down south.
A huge sea turtle—take a sledge hammer
to the massive shell, wedge it open

with one simple, solid blow
till the turtle can feel
no home above him, till everything
is taken away
and there is nothing
he will carry away from this moment.

My parents had three days
to relocate.
"Take only what you can carry."
One simple, solid blow—
They felt no home above them.

Dear Sirs:
Of course I'll come. I've packed my galoshes
and three packets of tomato seeds. Janet calls them
"love apples." My father says where we're going
they won't grow.

I am a fourteen-year-old girl with bad spelling
and a messy room. If it helps any, I will tell you
I have always felt funny using chopsticks
and my favorite food is hot dogs.
My best friend is a white girl named Denise—
we look at boys together. She sat in front of me
all through grade school because of our names:
O'Connor, Ozawa. I know the back of Denise's head very well.
I tell her she's going bald. She tells me I copy on tests.
We are best friends.

I saw Denise today in Geography class.
She was sitting on the other side of the room.
"You're trying to start a war," she said, "giving secrets away
to the Enemy, Why can't you keep your big mouth shut?"
I didn't know what to say.
I gave her a packet of tomato seeds
and asked her to plant them for me, told her
when the first tomato ripens
to miss me.

"We were sent to Jerome, Arkansas.
Arriving there, I wondered how long
we would be fenced in."

The nice thing about counting stars is
you can do it just about anywhere.
Even in a relocation camp
miles from home, even in Jerome, Arkansas
where a barbed wire fence crisscrosses itself
making stars of its own—but nothing
worth counting, nothing worth singing to.

My father remembers only two things:

> washing dishes in the mess hall each morning
> beside George Kaminishi and

> listening to Bing Crosby sing "White Christmas"
> on the radio in the barracks late at night.

One morning, George looked up from a greasy skillet
at my dad and said Yosh, you're a happy-go-lucky guy.
What do you want to do with your life?
It was the first time he realized he had a life
to do things with. He was fifteen. He didn't know.
It was only later that Dad found out George
had colon cancer and had no life to do things with.
And when Bing sang late at night that song
Dad could only think, He's not singing to me he's
singing to white people.

> "I'm dreaming of a white Christmas,
> just like the ones I used to know."

My mother meanwhile was in a different camp
and hadn't met my father. At night, she'd lie
in bed and think about the old family car
back in the driveway—were the windows smashed
and broken into, the thing driven away by thieves?

Or was the grass a foot tall now, erasing the
Goodyear tires that were so shiny and new?
There was a hole in the week where Sunday
used to be, and she *wanted* jelly bismarcks
more than ever.

> "Somehow we adjusted. There were weekly
> dances for the young. Dad sent away
> for a huge paper umbrella of vivid colors,

and Peg and I hugged it during the stormy
days."

Tonight, almost half a century later,
my father celebrates his 60th birthday.
He sits marking papers in the orange chair
in the living room, my mother enters grades
in the gradebook. In one corner
a brass gooseneck umbrella stand has been turned
into a planter—an ivy climbing its way
out. The oscillating fan shakes its head.

He remembers high school, Mrs. Barnett in Latin class,
himself at the head of it. A few days
before relocation, she took him aside.
So you'll be leaving us? she asked.
My father nodded.
She looked out the window at a maple tree
giving its leaves back to the earth,
at the chalky swirls of dust
on the blackboard for some good word
at the end of it all:

Look on it as an adventure, she said.

JANICE MIRIKITANI
Prisons of Silence

1.

The strongest prisons are built
with walls of silence.

2.

Morning light falls between us
like a wall.
We have laid beside each other

as we have for years.
Before the war, when life
would clamor through our windows,
we woke joyfully to the work.

I keep those moments
like a living silent seed.

After a day's work, I would
smell the damp soil in his hands,
his hands that felt the outlines
of my body in the velvet
night of summers.

I hold his warm hands to this
cold wall of flesh
as I have for years

3.

Jap!
Filthy Jap!

Who lives within me?

Abandoned homes, confiscated land,
loyalty oaths, barbed wire prisons
in a strange wasteland.

Go home, Jap!
Where is home?

A country of betrayal.
No one speaks to us.

We would not speak to each other.

We were accused.

Hands in our hair,
hands that spread our legs
and searched our thighs for secret weapons,
hands that knit barbed wire
to cripple our flight.

Giant hot hands flung me,
fluttering, speechless into
barbed wire, thorns in a broken wing.

The strongest prisons are built
with walls of silence.

4.

I watched him depart that day
from the tedious wall of wire,
the humps of barracks,
handsome in his uniform

I would look each day for letters
from a wall of time,
waiting for approach of my deliverance
from a wall of dust.

I do not remember
reading about his death
only the wall of wind
that encased me, as I turned my head.

5.

U.S. Japs hailed as heroes!

I do not know the face of this country
it is inhabited by strangers
who call me obscene names.

Jap. Go home.
Where is home?

I am alone wandering
in this desert.

Where is home?
Who lives within me?

A stranger with knife in her tongue
and broken wing,

mad from separations and losses cruel
as hunger.

Walls suffocate her as a tomb,
encasing history.

6.

I have kept myself contained
within these walls shaped to my body
and buried my rage.

I rebuilt my life
like a wall, unquestioning.
Obeyed their laws . . . their laws.

7.

All persons of Japanese ancestry
filthy jap.
Both alien and non-alien
japs are enemy aliens.
To be incarcerated
for their own good
A military necessity
The army to handle only the japs.
Where is home?
A country of betrayal.

8.

This wall of silence crumbles
from the bigness of their crimes.
This silent wall
crushed by living memory.

He awakens from the tomb
I have made for myself
and unearths my rage.

I must speak.

9.

He faces me in this small
room of myself.
I find the windows
where light escapes.

From this cell of history
this mute grave.

We heal our tongues.

We listen to ourselves

   Korematsu, Hirabayashi, Yasui.

We ignite the syllables of our names.

We give testimony.

We hear the bigness of our sounds freed
like many clapping hands,
thundering for reparations.

We give testimony.

Our noise is dangerous.

10.

We beat our hands
like wings healed.

We soar
from these walls of silence.

LAWSON FUSAO INADA

Rayford's Song

Rayford's song was Rayford's song,
but it was not his alone, to own.

He had it, though, and kept it to himself
as we rowed-rowed-rowed the boat
through English country gardens
with all the whispering hope
we could muster, along with occasional
choruses of funiculi-funicula!

Weren't we a cheery lot—
Comin' 'round the mountain
with Susanna, banjos on our knees,
rompin' through the leaves
of the third-grade music textbook.

Then Rayford Butler raised his hand.
For the first time, actually,
in all the weeks he had been in class,
and for the only time before he'd leave.
Yes, quiet Rayford, silent Rayford,
little Rayford, dark Rayford—
always in the same overalls—
that Rayford, Rayford Butler, raised his hand:

> "Miss Gordon, ma'am—
> we always singing your songs.
> Could I sing one of my own?"

Pause. We looked at one another;
We looked at Rayford Butler;
We looked up at Miss Gordon, who said:

> "Well, I suppose so, Rayford—
> if you insist. Go ahead.
> Just one song. Make it short."

And Rayford Butler stood up very straight,
and in his high voice, sang:

"Suh-whing ah-loooow,
suh-wheeet ah-charr-eee-oohh,
ah-comin' for to carr-eee
meee ah-hooooome . . ."

Pause. Classroom, school, schoolyard,
neighborhood, the whole world
focusing on that one song, one voice
which had a light to it, making even
Miss Gordon's white hair shine
in the glory of it, glowing
in the radiance of the song.

Pause. Rayford Butler sat down.
And while the rest of us
may have been spellbound,
on Miss Gordon's face
was something like a smile,
or perhaps a frown:

> "Very good, Rayford.
> However, I must correct you:
> the word is 'char*iot.*'
> 'Char*iot.*' And there is no
> such thing as a 'char*io.*'
> Do you understand me?

> "But Miss Gordon . . ."

> "I said 'char*iot*, char*iot.*'
> Can you pronounce that for me?"

> "Yes, Miss Gordon. Char*iot.*"

> "Very good, Rayford.
> Now class, before we return
> to our book, would anyone else
> care to sing a song of their own?"

Our songs, our songs, were there—
on tips of tongues, but stuck
in throats—songs of love,
fun, animals, and valor, songs
of other lands, in other languages,

but they just wouldn't come out.
Where did our voices go?

Rayford's song was Rayford's song,
but it was not his alone, to own.

"Well, then, class—
let's turn our books to
'Old Black Joe.'"

GARRETT HONGO
Four Chinatown Figures

In a back alley, on the cracked pavement slick with the strewn waste
of cooking oil and rotting cabbages, two lovers stroll arm in arm,
the woman in furs and a white lamé dress with matching pumps,
her escort in a tux casually worn—the black tie undone,
the double-breasted, brushed-velvet coat unbuttoned.
They're a Wilshire lawyer and city planner out on the town.
When they pass the familiar curio of the wishing well
with its Eight Immortals spouting aqueous wisdoms
through their copper mouths and baggy sleeves, they spend a minute
considering the impotent, green nozzle of its fountain.
The reflecting pool, speckled blue willow or streaked turquoise
as a robin's egg from the small litter of coins wintering on its bottom,
catches starlight and red neon in a tarn of winged ephemera
streaking across the black glaze of homely water. The lawyer
kisses his date and tosses some bus change, balls up
the foil wrapper from an after-dinner mint and throws that,
while she laughs, shaking her head back so the small,
mousse-stingered whips on the ringlets of her hair shudder
and dress sequins flash under the sore, yellow light of streetlamps.
Two dishwashers step from the back door of the Golden Eagle
arguing about pay, about hours, about trading green cards
with cousins for sex, set-ups with white women, for cigarettes
or a heated hotel room to sleep in on a dry, newspaper bed.
Bok-guai, they curse with their eyes, *Lo-fahn*, as the four nearly collide,
separate galaxies equal in surprise as they wheel to face each other.
The lawyer thinks little of these punks in T-shirts and Hong Kong jeans,

but the woman rhapsodizes, for no reason, in suspense/thriller prose—
slender and boylike, the bull's ring curl to their flimsy moustaches;
they must be cold in this dry, winter chill of late December in L.A.—
the sky a high velvet, indigo-to-black as it vaults, lazily,
from the city's fluorescent glow to the far azimuth
where the bear and huntsman drift casually into nothing.
Without jackets, the Chinese have bundled themselves in castoff,
cotton aprons stained with intricate patterns of lard and duck's blood
and wrapped like double-slings around their shoulders and folded arms.
Something grins on the face of the taller, fairer-complected one,
glints from his foxteeth, smolders in breathfog, camphor about to flare.
She tells herself, *Forget it, c'mom,* and, with a hooked finger,
snaps at the man's satin cummerbund. They turn away.
Without a gesture, in the greasy dark, the two Chonks turn away too,
back towards each other, and hear, quickening away behind them,
steps receding into the light din of street noise and sidewalk chatter.
The fair one says, audibly and in English, *Kiss me, white ghost,*
and, briefly staggered in the amniotic burst of light
from a passing tourist's flash, shrugs off his gruesome apron,
pulling out a pack of Gauloises, blue-wrapped, *especial,*
and strikes a match, holding it in the orange well of his hands
as, dragonlike, they both light up and puff, posed on a street vent,
hunching their thin shoulders and turning uptown against the wind.

The Legend

In Chicago, it is snowing softly
and a man has just done his wash for the week.
He steps into the twilight of early evening,
carrying a wrinkled shopping bag
full of neatly folded clothes,
and, for a moment, enjoys
the feel of warm laundry and crinkled paper,
flannellike against his gloveless hands.
There's a Rembrandt glow on his face,
a triangle of orange in the hollow of his cheek
as a last flash of sunset
blazes the storefronts and lit windows of the street.

He is Asian, Thai or Vietnamese,
and very skinny, dressed as one of the poor
in rumpled suit pants and a plaid mackinaw,

dingy and too large.
He negotiates the slick of ice
on the sidewalk by his car,
opens the Fairlane's back door,
leans to place the laundry in,
and turns, for an instant,
toward the flurry of footsteps
and cries of pedestrians
as a boy—that's all he was—
backs from the corner package store
shooting a pistol, firing it,
once, at the dumbfounded man
who falls forward,
grabbing at his chest.

A few sounds escape from his mouth,
a babbling no one understands
as people surround him
bewildered at his speech.
The noises he makes are nothing to them.
The boy has gone, lost
in the light array of foot traffic
dappling the snow with fresh prints.
Tonight, I read about Descartes'
grand courage to doubt everything
except his own miraculous existence
and I feel so distinct
from the wounded man lying on the concrete
I am ashamed.

Let the night sky cover him as he dies.
Let the weaver girl cross the bridge of heaven
and take up his cold hands.

In memory of Jay Kashiwamura

LAWSON FUSAO INADA

On Being Asian American

for our children

Of course, not everyone
can be an Asian American.
Distinctions are earned,
and deserve dedication.

Thus, from time of birth,
the journey awaits you—
ventures through time,
the turns of the earth.

When you seem to arrive,
the journey continues;
when you seem to arrive,
the journey continues.

Take me as I am, you cry,
I, I, am an individual.
Which certainly is true.
Which generates an echo.

Who are all your people
assembled in celebration,
with wisdom and strength,
to which you are entitled.

For you are at the head
of succeeding generations,
as the rest of the world
comes forward to greet you.

As the rest of the world
comes forward to greet you.

MICHAEL McCLURE
The Death of Kin Chuen Louie

NOW, ON THE DAY BEFORE MY DAUGHTER'S
TWENTY-FIRST BIRTHDAY,
ON THE AFTERNOON OF HER PARTY,
I REVISIT THE SCENE OF THE DEATH
of Kin Chuen Louie.
He too was between twenty and twenty-one.
The newspapers called him
a smalltime extortionist.
But what are we all but small
time extortionists in the
proportionless
universe?
(I am in awe of the thought
of the coolness and sureness
of his assassin.)
Twelve days ago, on the Festival
of the Lord Buddha, shortly
after two in the afternoon,
Kin Chuen Louie left his flat
on Kearney Street.
Louie's young, long-haired murderer,
in black jacket and army pants,
waited with a .380
Walther automatic pistol holding
fourteen bullets. Kin Chuen Louie,
spotting his assailant, leaped
into his bright red Plymouth Fury.
The murderer stepped
to the driver's side and fired a shot
into Louie. Louie started the ignition
and slammed into reverse.
His foot stuck on the accelerator.
The car, propelled backward with great
force, jammed between
a building and a white car
parked there — knocking loose shards
of red brick painted over with beige.
The murderer stepped quickly

to the passenger side of the trapped
and roaring car and fired seven bullets
through the windshield
into a tight pattern on the head and neck
of Louie. A ninth shot missed,
going finger-deep
into brick. The killer
fled a few yards, turned at the corner,
and disappeared down Sonoma Alley.
A moment later,
we arrived on the empty street
and looked through
shattered glass
at the young Chinese man —
blood pouring out of the holes
in his head — slumped over
on his side. It was like the close-up
in a Sam Peckinpah movie.
He was completely relaxed
— finally and almost pleasantly limp
and serene — wearing an army jacket
and grubby levis . . . a slender, handsome,
clean-cut face with short hair boyishly
hanging in his eyes above
the dime-size bullet holes.
The blood pouring onto the seat covers
was a thick, reddish vermillion.
There was a peaceful, robbe-grilletish,
dim light inside the car.
The shattered window was like
a frosted spider web.
Either death is beautiful to see
— or we learn the esthetic
of death from films. BUT I do know
that our physical, athletic body,
a thing of perfect loops, and secret
and manifest
dimensions and breathings of consciousness
and unconsciousness, emanates
rainbows and actions,
and black flowers
and it is there
to bear us through the world
and to kiss us goodbye at the doorstep

of any other.
I praise Everything-That-Is
for that blessing.
I drink chrysanthemum
tea in his memory.
Candied ginger, scented with licorice
from Hong Kong,
is on my breath.

I know each death

shall be as fine as his is.

LAWRENCE JOSEPH
Sand Nigger

In the house in Detroit
in a room of shadows
when grandma reads her Arabic newspaper
it is difficult for me to follow her
word by word from right to left
and I do not understand
why she smiles about the Jews
who won't do business in Beirut
"because the Lebanese
are more Jew than Jew,"
or whether to believe her
that if I pray
to the holy card of Our Lady of Lebanon
I will share the miracle.
Lebanon is everywhere
in the house: in the kitchen
of steaming pots, leg of lamb
in the oven, plates of kousa,
hushwee rolled in cabbage,
dishes of olives, tomatoes, onions,
roasted chicken, and sweets;
at the card table in the sunroom

where grandpa teaches me
to wish the dice across the backgammon board
to the number I want;
Lebanon of mountains and sea,
of pine and almond trees,
of cedars in the service
of Solomon, Lebanon
of Babylonians, Phoenicians, Arabs, Turks
and Byzantines, of the one-eyed
monk, Saint Maron,
in whose rite I am baptized;
Lebanon of my mother
warning my father not to let
the children hear,
of my brother who hears
and from whose silence
I know there is something
I will never know; Lebanon
of grandpa giving me my first coin
secretly, secretly
holding my face in his hands,
kissing me and promising me
the whole world.
My father's vocal cords bleed;
he shouts too much
at his brother, his partner,
in the grocery store that fails.
I hide money in my drawer, I have
the talent to make myself heard.
I am admonished to learn,
never to dirty my hands
with sawdust and meat.
At dinner, a cousin
describes his niece's head
severed with bullets, in Beirut,
in civil war. "More than
an eye for an eye," he demands,
breaks down, and cries.
My uncle tells me to recognize
my duty, to use my mind,
to bargain, to succeed.
He turns the diamond ring
on his finger, asks if

I know what asbestosis is,
"the lungs become like this,"
he says, holding up a fist;
he is proud to practice
law which "distributes
money to compensate flesh."
Outside the house my practice
is not to respond to remarks
about my nose or the color of my skin.
"Sand nigger," I'm called,
and the name fits: I am
the light-skinned nigger
with black eyes and the look
difficult to figure—a look
of indifference, a look to kill—
a Levantine nigger
in the city on the strait
between the great lakes Erie and St. Clair
which has a reputation
for violence, an enthusiastically
bad-tempered sand nigger
who waves his hands, nice enough
to pass, Lebanese enough
to be against his brother,
with his brother against his cousin.
with cousin and brother
against the stranger.

Not Yet

When my father breathed
unevenly I breathed
unevenly, I prayed
in St. Maron's Cathedral
for the strength
of a cedar tree
and for the world to change.
When I saw my father's tears
I did not pray;
I hated our grocery store
where the bullet

barely missed his heart,
I hoped the mist exhaled
by the Vale of Esk
in a country of lakes
4,000 miles away
would be mine.
That was before
Lopez whispered through his rotten teeth
behind a maze of welding guns,
"You're colored, like me,"
before I knew
there is so much
anger in my heart,
so much need
to avenge the holy cross
and the holy card
with its prayers for the dead,
so many words
I have no choice to say.
Years without enough to make me
stop talking!
I want it all.
I don't want
the angel inside me, sword in hand,
to be silent.
Not yet.

Then

Joseph Joseph breathed slower
as if that would stop
the pain splitting his heart.
He turned the ignition key
to start the motor and leave
Joseph's Food Market to those
who wanted what was left.
Take the canned peaches,
take the greens, the turnips,
drink the damn whiskey
spilled on the floor,
he might have said.

Though fire was eating half
Detroit, Joseph could only think
of how his father,
with his bad legs, used to hunch
over the cutting board
alone in light particled
with sawdust behind
the meat counter, and he began
to cry. Had you been there
you would have been thinking
of the old Market's wooden walls
turned to ash or how Joseph's whole arm
had been shaking as he stooped
to pick up an onion,
and you would have been afraid.
You wouldn't have known
that soon Joseph Joseph would stumble,
his body paralyzed an instant
from neck to groin.
You would simply have shaken your head
at the tenement named "Barbara" in flames
or the Guardsman with an M-16
looking in the window of Dave's Playboy Barbershop,
then closed your eyes
and murmured, This can't be.
You wouldn't have known
it would take nine years
before you'd realize the voice howling in you
was born then.

DIANE ABU-JABER
Arabs and the Break in the Text

A break in the text falls like a blow to the chest. Or a lull in the storm: shelter against the words that rain against the eyes. Writers take the internal storm by its tail, like Paul Bunyan grasping the tail of the cyclone.

Then there is physical violence, that first stunning blow, that leaves you breathless, shocked by assault. If you are a woman, the attacker's hands are often the more powerful. You are lifted, you are thrown.

Time goes elastic, the world disintegrates into lights, colors that run; it is the world of visceral pain, waves between the teeth, the back of the head, against the ribs. The body attempts to collapse inward, but there is no collapsing point: you were born into a world that is not safe for you.

In the early seventies, at what must have been the peak of the decade's energy crisis, my family moved to a small town in upstate New York. My father painted the big, rural mailbox coal black, and from nearly half a mile off, you could read the 3-inch high cherry-red "ABU-JABER" that he'd painted on both sides. The kids who shared the hour-long bus ride to school with me lived in abandoned farms houses and barns; their whole families squatted in dilapidated ruins without electricity or water.

All that the kids on the bus knew about Arabs came from the same educational sources that served most of America: TV, Hollywood, political cartoons, so they knew that Arabs were dark men, hook-nosed and beetle-browed, with white sheets and greasy fingers. They knew that Arabs were responsible for the energy crisis; the reason why they were cold at home. And hungry. And why their parents fought and drank and ran away, or stayed and beat them.

That bus ride was a five year conference in hate. They were children; they said and did what people attempt to conceal when they grow up. Thirty young people, voices tapped from their parents, speaking from the belly of America.

The violence of that time is something that I was able to squeeze and forge into a black store of secrets. I keep it as my own souvenir.

There is the violence that comes from outside, then there is the frightening violence from the interior. The boundary between in and out dissolves; there is no hiding place, not your own hearth, not your own heart.

My whole family felt the anger. We lived in a world cleft as a devil's hoof, split by the colonist's dark dream of "East" and "West."

The first-generation children of our family enabled and embodied the struggle that went on between our American grandmother and our Arab father. Ostensibly, they fought over us, over our loyalties and identities. But the family stories suggest the fight went farther back, to the glances behind my American mother's bridal gown, the piece of paper my Moslim father had to sign, swearing to rear us as Catholics, as he stood among the pews full of good Catholics with raised eyebrows.

Years later, I found a newspaper clipping from the 1970s, tucked away and forgotten in the back of one of my grandmother's drawers. It was headlined, "The Arab Mind Lashed by Shame and Rage" and summed up its subject as follows, "The Arab possesses every human flaw and fault, but to an exaggerated degree."

It was such an outstanding piece of journalistic xenophobia that I saved it, intending to preserve it for future examination. Then I promptly mislaid it. Done in the same way, I suppose, people mislay the memories of assault and trauma.

What was perhaps most terrible about it, though, was not that a reporter in some distant newsroom believed this, but that the bile had spilled through the walls of my own grandmother's home. That she had clipped and saved it.

It spills through walls and windows, TV screens, and car windows, the violence flashes in gestures, words, and evasions. The hatred eats through everything like an acid, worst of all when it starts from the inside.

Lighten the hair, thin the lips, change the name, cover the dress, hammer down the accent, stash away the strange gods, the poetry, the ancient disturbing pointless old stories. Smash it all down flat.

When I was a graduate student, a professor told me to change my name. "Otherwise," he said. "You'll get pegged as some kind of *ethnic* writer."

During my job hunt for a teaching position, I walked into room after identical room, and watched faces fall as I failed to meet the expectations raised by my name. I am not black.

Today the name is on my office door. But I still hear it in the mouths of the children on the bus. I remember my family name, which means father of the healer, of the teacher, of the medicine worker, being turned into a hate chant.

Adults are not supposed to chew over the violences of childhood. So what a shock it is when we go through the arduous process of trying to *let go*, to reclaim the sanctuary of forgiveness, the power of maturity, only to find that the very air around us is singed by violence. We fly our common flag together, hands clapped over heart, pledge a common oath, so when the violence comes, it's no less a betrayal than a parent's abandonment.

When I won a local talent-beauty contest (desperate for money) I was handed a bouquet of roses and a tiara, so that as I and all the other contestants were being stripped of dignity, the violence posed as reward. When later on, again desperate, I did a brief stint writing pornography, I began to see the faces of my female characters staring at me over the backs of their partners, as if I were looking into a warped mirror. I realized that this country spared little love for its women, and that I'd somehow let that coldness into myself.

Some of us avert our eyes from that warped mirror, not to see the violence against women or minorities. Some people will say there is no intrinsic prejudice against Arabs in this country. Some will say, as one person once complained about a story of mine, why can't you write about the joy in life?

Once, in Winter of 1988, as a way of celebrating the joy and richness of Arabic culture, I invited a group of four Arab-American women to speak on a radio show that I produced in Ann Arbor, Michigan. They were there, in part, to discuss the Western portrayal of Arab men as bullies with scimitars and harems. The women openly addressed their struggle for gender equality within the Middle East and their struggle for cultural respect inside America. Because their culture, as one Palestinian woman said, was not only beautiful, but was also identity, especially for those in exile.

The next day when I walked into my office on campus, I noticed the floor crunched under my foot. I went in and saw the surface of my desk was glittering white. When I put out my hand I realized that I was surrounded by broken glass.

I found the rock in the corner, still wrapped in its message: "This to Palestinian Supporters."

When my sister asked my father why he wouldn't move to California, he said, in accented English, "Too many foreigners." The joke he told was on himself; as Nietzche explains, a joke is an epitaph on the death of a feeling.

The death of feeling comes slowly, in profound and tidal movements. Sometimes it requires a lifetime of pain and violence. After the first blow takes your breath away, pain slowly becomes a familiar place, even a home. k.d. laing sings, "A family tradition / the strength of this land / where what's right and wrong / is the back of a hand."

I have not lost the feeling, instead, it has grown strong and quiet. A lifetime of violence against women and Arabs has bred an anger in me that is difficult and complex in the ways that I experience it, the ways that I let it show. I feel my pen's ink spill like gunpowder from a powderkeg. The words ignite spontaneously. For me, there is no other way.

PETER ORESICK
Poem for Hamid

The political backdrop of this poem—written in 1980—is the Iranian revolution, the subsequent storming of the U.S. Embassy, and the long captivity of American hostages there. At that time Islamic fundamentalists, led by Ayatollah Khomeni, consolidated their power and persecuted democratic and left forces, driving many into hiding.

In Pittsburgh, as an activist in a grassroots organization on the Middle East, I worked with several Iranians and Arabs with relatives in hiding. One night that winter, Hamid and I posted leaflets publicizing a conference on the Palestine question. We were arrested and spent the night in jail. I wrote this poem to continue our on-going discussion about the contradictions of life in North America for third-worlders and first-worlders.

I.

Dawn: the sky whitens.
All night the blue factories clanked & whirred,
thickening the air.
Yet this is a morning,
and this is a grapefruit, this sugar.
This is a key, a car; this is torque
and we move.

This is North America. Have a nice day.
This is not hell, it's a supermarket
See the lettuce: bib, leaf, iceberg, romaine.
This is not death, it's fried chicken.
Taste it. It has taste.

2. LETTER FROM ABROAD, MAY 1981

The left disappears. Many are underground and the prisons are full.
Some mornings the gunshots wake us. Fadwa will rush out of bed,
dress, chatter about getting work, but I linger. I am writing leaflets,
translating, smoking too much. No word yet from Ali. Mother
worries and busies herself cooking.

3.

Remember the time we were taken to jail?
Posting leaflets illegally.
Getting out by morning—my only concern—
while you were lost in study:
how two kids in for robbery paced,
how they couldn't fill out the forms.

Drunk or dumb? What did it matter?
I think of the green walls peeling
the one toilet, the chill that floated in
from the hall.
What makes you believe
everyone lives to some purpose?

4.

That is my son
pulling himself up on the chair leg.
That is his world, *bup*, sailing
in this comfortable room.
What here is not to like?
What?

5. LETTER FROM ALI, JULY 1981

I am living in a northern province. No running water, no electricity,
nothing like the undergraduate life I loved in Denver. The new
regime has no influence here. I am hidden by a good family; from
my window I watch them going about each day. The women must
knock away shit with a stick before drawing water. Crops are poor.
Oil does us little good without rainfall. Some days I wonder how
we'll change what the centuries have not touched.

6.

Hamid, that your grief were my life
or my life your grief, is academic.
The lawn fertilizer I do not buy

may never reach your country.
We do what we can. No regrets.
This is still a life, not grief.
Still life.

JOYCE CAROL OATES
There Was A Shot

and then silence, except for screams he didn't hear
since he was concentrating on walking, and
walking, he knew not to falter in his stride since
momentum carries us forward, and not logic,
nor even strength.

He was crossing West Huron, the traffic lights were swaying,
and he was too distracted to notice the trickling down
his legs, warm, and sudden, and shameful as urine,
his socks and his shoes are already soaked, a wild
itching in his gut, his bellybutton aflame.

He was in motion, he was aware that that's the trick,
not to stumble at the curb like a drunk, though the curb
is higher than he'd expected, and West Huron wider, O God
now's not the time to hesitate, nor even to glance down
to what's dragging at his feet.

He was waxy in the face, he was using his arms as paddles,
he was floating, he was sinking, he was ignoring the red
splotches on the pavement like coins falling from his pockets,
he was three blocks from home and didn't know his name
and he was preparing to laugh it off, and even forgive.

He was ignoring the faces, and he wasn't hearing the voices,
and when we touched him he wrenched away, the trick is just
to move one foot in front of the other, that's the primary trick
from which all others follow, not to falter, not to break
your stride, not to glance down, oh never.

What's a wild shot on a Saturday night, a stray bullet
from a skidding car, what's *accident*, but nobody's at fault,

make the best of a bad thing he knew so he was telling
this story to anyone willing to listen, once he got to
where he was going, and they knew him.

DAVID IGNATOW
The Faithful One

Praying, he moves among those holding knives.
He has been cut and does not mind now.
The air is noisy, the crowds large.
He moves or is pushed, no thrust
directly aimed at him. Swaying
or knocked aside, he feels no pain,
no weakening from loss of blood.
Who sees him turn astonished,
and turns quickly back to his blade.
Is there one who from mere pleasure
will thrust him dead?
He walks, faithful.

MICHAEL BLUMENTHAL
Stones

There are men and women who have thrown stones
and who can blame them?—
What else is a poet to do
in a world with so little use for him?

But I have always hated stones
and loved words,
and held to the deep illusion
that words could wound and heal
as no stones can, that one day
there will be a revolution of words
in which the angels will come

to sing with the vipers,
and even the dark flames of greed
will be doused by the right syllables
spoken in the right place.

But now I can see
that the thieves have broken in here too
and have stolen our words
and are trying to use them against us
in the name of greed
and in the name of power
and in the name of lust.

Yet I am still a man
in love with words
and does not want to throw stones.

So I merely go on,
hurling my beautiful words
against the warehouses and windows
of darkness and domination,
hoping some less timid soul than I am
will pick them up
and turn them into stones.

III. THE SCARS OF WAR

Cry *peace!* if you will
There is in the plasm the mood that denies it
There is in the fist the love of the striking,
And out of the heart the savage inviolate flame.
Life come to it shining: grass choking,
    the wolves slashing.
Napoleon, nor Caesar, nor Ghengis could have
    led the hordes,
Unwilling, into the jaws. They ran down singing.
And I who hold the poor dream as passionately
    as any,
Expect it never. We have sprung from the loins
    of that mother, the past,
And got something but love from her dugs.

—WILLIAM EVERSON

from "On the Anniversary of The Versailles Peace, 1936"

CLARENCE MAJOR

In Hollywood with the Zuni God of War

" . . . movie people. They all seemed quite mad." —Peggy Guggenheim

I

"It's as fake as Zuni
           jewelry made in Taiwan,"
I heard him
      tell the director
and that he was Zuni, and to his disgust
in Culver
      City cops called him Chief.
I was playing a mysterious dark role:
            not a speaking part.
We were in the Cochise movie
    and this is what Zugowa
          pointed at, as
he spoke.
      Director bit no tongue:
        Do ya wanna wok or not?

An Italian dude played Cochise.
Apache guy on set told director
           where to go, too.
Nearly got us all fired; set closed.
        Producers came down, frowning.
The script was all
      about the capture of Cochise.
Zugowa and the Apache tried
to point out to the director
    that he should start
with the white men whipping
           Chief Mangas Coloradas
because that's where Cochise
gets his anger—his motivation!
Talk about motivation in Hollywood!
      Director told us all,
go get laid in Burbank.
    what ya guys want?
      Ya got Studio City by da balls!

Ya got all the blondes
in the District hot fa ya
'cause ya got dok skin and ah—
Anyway, Coloradas struck
back   and the white men killed him.
They say the whole
Apache Nation rose
and this is where Cochise
of the Chiricahua comes in,
but the director
wasn't interested, He started his movie
with a bunch of anglo cowboys
galloping
across
a phony southwestern landscape
raising a cloud of dust
trying to track down
Cochise.
Cochise, you see, before the flick
kicks off, has been accused of killing
little Mickey Free
(we never learn that Cochise
is innocent,
and later, that he wipes
out forty before capture. You see
two fall)
I saw Cochise hiding; Zugowa
said, "there, away in the hills, but
why isn't he holding them off?"
till he's captured, but
you don't see the army losses, you instead
suffer like the ache in Big Eyes'
knuckles when he drew maps
for Coronado.

||

It was during the time when
everybody was hot and bothered
by that Mexican laborer
who killed this Indian
over a quarter
which the Indian dropped

in a jukebox
to play an Elvis Presley song,
    in other words—
You know what he said?
    "What ya got against Elvis?"

Zugowa was in one about
                a stagecoach robbery.
I sat on the sideline singing
    about Dat-So-La-Lee, watching,
chewing sage to keep my breath—
    blessed pollenway!—Yuccasweet.
All the Indians were wiped out.
    I saw it in L.A. Without prayer-
meal! The audience loved it!

I was in the Tomassa one,
        Zugowa wasn't. I got shot
in the first scene. A daylight person,
    I turned into a Shutsina—
Zugowa was in the Pocahontas
(silly, silly, silly . . .) thing,
A remake of the forties sentiment.
        ("it cannot be helped;
                we do not have the same
road," Bunzel quoted Lena
                Zuni.
Yo-a!
        No tcakwaina mana, this
Pocahontas! Break the piki
            in her honor! She was good.
said the anglos, 'cause
            she saved the life
of one of their own. Two? I forget.

"They did not care
            which tribe we came from."
Zugowa swore this was true
    in the name of Awonawilona,
            by his own mili.
We all looked alike.
    Being herded and shot
paid better than oranges in S.D.

County,
or the H.D. in Arizona—that is,
   if you could get yourself shot
at least once
          per month.
A liberal producer
   from back east wanted to make
a flick on Cherokee Gatumlati till
    somebody told him she was half
Negro. Studio pulled the plug
     out of his oxygen tent:
     white audiences in the South
might not buy it.

You might think that because Hopoekaw
         was married to a French officer
she was safe territory, but—

      Hooooooooo thlaiaaaa!

Me and Zugowa tried to get the director
    to eat etawa and yepna.
He left our table gagging.
    Heads in the cafeteria turned,
faces turned red.

We offered him queens,
       Cofachiqui and Pamunkey
   and royalty—Adell C.,
and twisted the arm of Joe Tipp,
    the token,
        but we got back "how
many times" etc., and the business
   about "point-of-view"
and audience demands.
    "Flick like that won't fly!"

III

. . . and this Navajo hombre said
           why
   did the Navajo

144

need a Bilagaana—must have
            been Kit Carson's face!
        or did your ancestors screw
that many blue-eyed settlers?
                        and the black gods?
What's with the black gods—
                        Bitsiislizhims?
        And you say we shot down
our black savior!
            He was no savior, Saiya!
                        You drink too much!

. . . and he said, We had Yellow Body.
        Calling God.
        Toninili.
        Water Sprinkler.
Zugowa had a friend at Saint Anthony's
            whose name was Bilagaana.
Imagine that! Know nothing
        about Blue Body. You keep thinking
            "me" and some kinda studio-lot-priest!
        (. . . bartender is sympathetic.)
Ahhh, the curse of Haashcheeshzini
                is henceforth upon you!
"Ready?"
        "Yes, yes! Altseasdzaa!"

IV

Ooooaaaioooo!
        Hoootaa hoooota!
                    . . . the movie about Sacajawea,
the so-called Bird-Woman of the Shoshones.
        You
know the story. Ya know it?

"—but they [Lewis and Clark] would
        have lost their direction
                without a compass."

Mother of Chief Quahhah,
        Cynthia Ann Parker,

of the Comanches—was proposed
      to the director by a group
of intelligent feminists. He shaved
      his finger at them.
They got the point.

Zugowa and me farmed out
          parking cars in South
L.A. when the Emily-thing
        got the okay
from the lot office.
      This jerk-off lieutenant
who's obviously been pumping her,
      marries a girl of the garrison.
Poor Emily, poor, poor Emily!
Emily, the stupid Indian
      "gal" who's shot by a sentry
as she sneaks back
   to warn the garrison of a planned
          Indian attack.
Last straw!
      The director told us
we were fools to
      jockey autos for peanuts
and tips from the crust! when
      we could ride high
   in the saddle under the big sky!

SHARON OLDS
The End of World War One

Out of the scraped surface of the land
men began to emerge, like puppies
from the slit of their dam. Up from the trenches
they came out upon the pitted, raw earth
wobbling as if new-born.
They could not believe they would be allowed to live;
the orders had come down: no more killing.
They approached the enemy, holding out chocolate

and cigarettes. They shook hands, exchanged
souvenirs—mess-kits, neckerchiefs.
Some even embraced, while in London
total strangers copulated
in doorways and on the pavement, in the ecstasy
of being reprieved. Nine months later,
like men emerging from trenches, first the head,
then the body, there were lifted, newborn, from these mothers,
the soldiers of World War Two.

DAVE SMITH
Leafless Trees, Chickahominy Swamp

Humorless, hundreds of trunks, gray in the blue expanse
where dusk leaves them hacked like a breastwork,
stripped like pikes planted to impale, the knots
of vines at each groin appearing placed by makers
schooled in grotesque campaigns. Mathew Brady's
plates show them as they are, the ageless stumps,
timed-sanded solitaries, some clumped in squads
we might imagine veterans, except they're only wood,
and nothing in the world seems more dead than these.

Stopped by the lanes filled with homebound taillights,
we haven't seen the rumored Eagle we hoped to watch,
only a clutch of buzzards ferrying sticks for a nest.
Is this history, that we want the unchanged, useless
spines out there to thrust in our faces the human
qualities we covet? We read this place like generals
whose promised recruits don't show, who can't press on:
we feel the languor of battle, troops unable to tell
themselves from the enemy, and a file-hard fear gone

indifferent in the mortaring sun that will leave all
night after night standing in the same cold planes
of water. It never blooms or greens. It merely stinks.
Why can't we admit this is death's gift, the scummy
scene of our pride, blown brainpans of a century ago?
Who do we sit and sniff the rank hours inside words

blunt as ground that only stares off our question: what
happened? Leaf-light in our heads, don't we mean why
these grisly emblems, the slime that won't swell to hope?

The rapacious odor of swamps all over the earth bubbles
sometimes to mist, fetid flesh we can't see but know
to be cells composing, decomposing, a heart's illusions.
God knows what we'd do in there, we say, easing back
on the blacktop. Once we heard a whistling. Harmonicas?
But who'd listen? Surely all was green once, fragile
as a truce, words braiding sun and water, as on a lake
where families sang. What else would we hope for, do
in the dead miles nothing explains or changes or relieves?

SAMUEL CHARTERS
Of Those Who Died:
A Poem of the Spring of 1945

I

Of those who died
        I knew so little.
They had been only voices,
    voices in a conversation,
only faces that I looked up into
        as the men sat thin and sunburned
in the stuffy rooms
            talking to someone else.
            I was too young—
only three years younger than they were,
    four,
        but I was younger, and I
wasn't like them. If, in the hallway,
I clumsily tried on their caps
        the dull olive drab sagged down
                over my forehead like peeling skin.
Their jackets hung from my shoulders
        like a question I didn't understand.

In the hallway's dim mirror
I only saw myself.
      I wasn't like them.
I was younger by the step they
  had taken through a doorway where I
couldn't follow,
    and I stood waiting uneasily
for them to return.

Their laughter
    was a kind of performance
      as they sat in thick palms
of stuffed chairs
       talking to their worried families,
to their worried girls.
      They always laughed,
as if laughter had once been taken away
from them
      and now they'd been given
bags of it that they strewed around the room,
     draping each other with it
like streamers,
    and every day had become a
desperate celebration.
      But even with shirts open, ties
pulled loose, their uniforms still marked them,
  still said they could be killed,
    and I knew them so little
I had to be told, slowly, which face,
     which voice, I should rub out
   of the loose sketch I had in my mind
   of the ones I knew.

But trying to rub out the faces
     of the ones who were killed
left only the reverse of the impression
      somewhere inside me,
and I still had glimpses of their faces,
    that I only half remembered,
and of their deaths,
    that I only half understood.
    What could it mean to me
      that someone I'd known—a laughing voice—
     was rolling face down

somewhere on the sand
    while the sea prodded him
        with its cat's paws.
How could I understand?
           How could I understand?

I couldn't understand,
      but I could forget.
I saw a man struggling up the school steps,
      his legs dragging after him with the
         stiffness of an insect
as his arms pulled him up,
      and forgetting, forgetting
his wounds from the Pacific
I said,
    "Hurt yourself over the weekend?"
And his white, set, contorted face
turned to me
       like an animal in pain
     and his eyes, staring at me,
       were livid with hate.

They walked away,
       they left me alone
in the hallway listening to sounds
that I didn't understand,
      touching decorations on uniforms
that didn't fit me,
      and sometimes I tried to
go after them,
       to turn at the end of the hallway
    where they turned,
     run down the stairs after them
         to the street,
but when I got to the sidewalk
       it was always empty.
They had gone somewhere
     I couldn't follow.

II

     What do I feel now
when I see their faces in the discoloring

distance of photographs,
                    as tense, as apprehensive
as small animals in a cage?
            What do I see in those
surprised eyes,
        what do I hear from those thin, pressed mouths?
I can almost hear them talking,
                    see their lips move—
        but instead of words
            I only hear the words of the songs
        they sang as they clung to their girls
at dances. Lipstick stains on wrinkled shirts
as heads pressed against shoulders, hips stiffly
            crushed against hips.
        Even I, standing nervously watching,
                could hear the songs.
It was always the same song,
            it always said the same thing,
                even when the words, or the song,
were different.
"Kiss me once and kiss me twice
and kiss me once again,
it's been a long, long time . . ."
            And part of the stiffness as they danced
in their wrinkled uniforms
                    was their fear,
and their fear became part of the song,
            as close to them, and as elusive
        as insects
            caught in amber's unending sunset.

        I could sense the song
                in the photographs of their faces.
It was there, a sound, just beyond the edge
            of the frame.
A customer at my afternoon job at Schiller's Pharmacy
        was a young wife who sat for an hour
            every day at a table,
        her desperation as conspicuous as a statue.
She was at that moment when her body
                yearned to bear,
            and she trembled with its yearning like
                someone pressing against
a wind that wasn't there, that pulled at her

clothes, that mussed her hair.
           As I watched her she drank
the Coca Cola I brought her with an intensity
           that sagged from her shoulders
                         like a tear,
and her fingers twined, untwined on the
table's glass top,
           twined, twisted at the ring
on her finger.
        Twisting it as if she'd pull it off,
twisting it
           as if she'd force it on more tightly.

           Seersucker dresses, skirts creased
from the heat
           that sifted through the opened door,
her stockingless legs brown from days
              empty of everything but sun,
        her hair combed, but her lips left plain.
Her body crouched in its hunger
              as if she were forcing herself
                  not to run from the table.
But she waited the months out
           like someone marking off the hours in a cell,
              and one day on the street
I saw her walking slowly with the red-faced,
           limping man who was her husband,
and the wind had died.
Nothing was pulling at her,
           and her hair was tied with a ribbon
        that held it close to her head
with the softness of breath.
"Kiss me once and kiss me twice . . ."

           And I heard the song's whispered lines
in the flaccid, rumpled body of a woman
           swaying against the stale smells
of a stained seat across a train aisle from me,
         her hair straggling into
            small groping strings down her
      perspiring neck,
               her eyes rimmed with dark
fingers of shadow.
           Her body was as heavy

with its hungers,
     but the uneasy spread of her legs
said that she, unlike the other woman,
   was helpless against it.
                Three soldiers in uniforms
as fingered as the train seats
        sat with her, one beside her,
    the others helping her drink.
"I'm married to a fly boy, you know,"
she whined in a voice that seemed to look
at itself
    in the dirty mirror of the sounds
          around them,
"He was shipping out and all and I didn't think
    we ought to wait so we got married.
He's got a leave coming in a month."
A month, a month,
        but at this moment, with the dying
sunlight spewing itself over
         the dirt of Colorado,
her body was slipping helplessly
    through her fingers.
It wasn't a wind that was pressing against her,
   tangling her clothes, her hair,
         it was a flood
    that was carrying her out,
turning her over in its swirling current.
"He's just done his year's tour so he's getting
three weeks and we can have us a little
honeymoon together."
        The arm on her shoulder
    was a question, the unshaven face
   of the soldier leaning against her
        was a question.
"I thought I'd come out and get us a
    room in L.A. or Long Beach,
and wait for him to get there."

The smell of whiskey rind, the days
    in the train strewn on the floor
   in twisted shreds
of cigarets, the fingers of her hair
trailing down her neck,
   the soldier's

fingers like a vein spreading
over the sagging weight of her breast.
"My husband
    gets back stateside next month . . ."
        the whining voice no one
                    was listening to,
    "Thought I'd get out early, you know,
and hunt something up."
The flood rising around her in the
            last, heavy, yellowing breath
of sunset.

            The train shaking as it fumbled
over a switchpoint,
                    the eyes around her glittering
        as the light sieved into darkness.
        Her voice thinning, whiskey licked
from fingers as paper cups leaked,
            the current pushing at her,
            prodding her.
                        In the stifled darkness
under a huddled blanket
            on the slow slope to the New Mexico
state line
        she and the soldier beside her
managed a kind of convulsive coupling,
                    and I watched their
            bodies heave
over and over again in a raging,
            lurching movement as the current
        tore them, rolled them, pulled them
down into its heaving eddies,
                until with a drunken mewing
I heard her dragged under.

        An aimless pushing of shadows
as the morning came into the car
    and made its way down the aisle
a seat at a time.
            A low droning of sleep
from the woman sprawled open mouthed now
on the seat across from me,
                clothes rumpled,
pulled loose under the blanket's sweat,

skin dirtied, a half-opened eye
reddening with the sun's reflection,
            the skin grainy, lips burning
as the train
            fled from the cruelty of the flaccid
yellow dawn into New Mexico.
            With a voice like a torn sleeve
                she asked for a cup of coffee.

I couldn't talk to the men
            who were going to die,
        I couldn't talk to the desperate,
yearning women they left behind them.
            They had taken a few steps
        away from me and I could see them
    as they stood talking in the half light.
The only thing I could understand
            from the movement of their lips
        were the words to their songs.
"Kiss me once and kiss me twice
and kiss me once again . . ."

III

There was no face to the death
            that was waiting for them there—
                only a distance to it that
they crossed with feet that dragged
                heavier and heavier
        as they drew closer.
But for those of us
    who could only see it from far away
it had less than a face,
            it had less than a body.
        There was nothing to it
    that could be touched or felt.
            But I knew that it happened—
that it was happening.
                And sometimes I would
imagine it, like images from an old film
that had become scratched
                from too much use.
One death came back to me again

and again and again
and I imagined it
again and again and again—
the death of the pilots
down over the Pacific—the pilots whose ships
were lost,
and who dropped into the water
searching, searching for some place
they could rest.

Were they calm? Did they dream?
What did they do in those hours?
"I looked for someplace
to come down," says one, in greasy overalls
and goggles pushed up on his forehead,
"I looked and looked and when
the engine finally died I thought
it was a blue field
I was falling into—
and I was going to get out
and walk around,
then something tapped me
on the shoulder,
and it was the blue water
coming in to sit beside me."
"I wrote letters,"
says another one with flopping cap
over his ears,
"on my clipboard, on the pages
of instructions for checking the instruments
in case of emergencies. I wrote my wife.
I started, 'Dear Ruth, I don't know if you'll
ever get this letter, but I wanted to let you know
how much I'm thinking of you now. Honey, this
might be the last chance I'll have to tell you . . .'
The rest is personal," he says, staring away
with eyes as distant
as the emptiness beyond the moon.
"Just at the last
I thought I was as natural as a bird,"
says another, with a smudge of oil
on his forehead,
where he'd wiped the sweat off with his thumb,
"I thought I could keep right on going,

and when the needle showed up dry
I just pulled back and I went up, up,
  letting the wind carry me
        one more time, looking one
    more time around the horizon
and it was as naked as a baby's stomach,
        and just then the wind
      opened its fingers
            and let me fall."

        The droning of the planes haunted me,
the frantic buzzing,
        like flies trapped in a closed room,
      the sound weakening, dying until
I could hear it in my sleep.
          It was the emptiness
      of it that picked with insistent fingers
at my dreams.
          It was always the circle of the
horizon that I saw,
      that drew its barren ring
around my shut eyes, and drifting
toward it was the silver, droning shape
            of the plane.
The pilot tired now, from turning
      in the cramped seat, tired now
from crying into the radio
        that only buzzed back
its own stillness,
          the silence stretched so tightly
      against the skin
that it drew blood.
Hands that had clutched at the controls
        had loosened,
        tears had dried.
              The ocean, in a rim,
    hung in front of him
            and the plane
  pushed dully toward it,
    with only a weak line of cloud
ahead of him,
        which was death,
      only a reddening, flaring

ball of sun gaping up
    out of the streaming ocean's edge
behind him,
                which was death,
            only the feeling of the ache
        in his moistureless mouth,
in his burning eyes,
                    which was death.

And the choking cough
            as the engine shuddered still
        woke me,
            and I lay staring up into the darkness,
listening to the last soughing
        of the dying wings
                    as they fell.

IV

                But when the world turned over
on its back again, and the time for war
came around again,
                and I followed them into
the uniforms they'd just taken off—
        I found only the ordinariness of it.
With my old clothes stuffed into a new
                khaki laundry bag I stared out of the
    barracks window onto the trampled
patch of withered grass asking myself,
"Is this what it was like? It this what
                they were like?"
                    Sometimes,
pulling off a sweaty shirt, rubbing salve
        on bruises, I looked up,
I thought I saw faces that were their faces.
Sitting on the ribbed bench of a truck
                        I turned to look into
a bus parked close to us on a strip
of pavement in the company area—
                and it was the faces I'd seen before.
        I started to open a window, to say
something to them,

but the evolutions of time only
enclose themselves
within each other,
they don't intersect.
The doors closed with a metal clang,
the bus started, their faces
disappeared.

It was the ordinariness of it,
the monotony of it that stayed with us.
As if we were all standing in the same
water soaked ditch, digging with the
same shovel that we passed back and forth
to each other,
its handle sweaty from
each other's hands.
Only someone who had never done it
could have said something about
these hallowed deaths, or someone
who didn't understand it could relate it
either to patriotism or disillusionment,
to any slogans or causes.
Pretensions of intellect which, at least,
we were without.

In a room years later,
together with uncles, my father, cousins,
I only felt our ordinariness.
Six of us, standing in the kitchen drinking,
a sound of women's voices
from the other room
as we talked.
Our ordinariness—but the
uncle leaning against the refrigerator, hair graying,
face still red with the sun,
under his shirt his body
marked with a splay of machine gun bullets.
The cousin laughing at something his father
has said,
laughing in a voice with its own
darkness,
one lung torn away by a land mine.
The rest of us, except for his brother,

unmarked on skin or bodies,
but the marks left
somewhere within us,
Our ordinariness, which we felt
comfortable in, like an old shirt we kept
to wear around the house,
but the uncle with the scribble
of bullets in him—
thirty years service—
the uncle beside me, bearded now and with eyes
sad with old resolutions,
twenty years. Two uncles not here,
but we talk of them,
one in meaningless duty—
was it in Seattle?—the other a
pilot, one for two, the other three years.
A cousin, the shorter, darker brother
of the cousin who lost the lung,
two years—myself, two years—
only my father, working in a shipyard,
left out of it.
The ordinariness of one family,
without fervor, without heroics,
but between the seven of us
sixty-one years of service.
What was worth these sixty-one years
of our lives?
What did our families get
from these sixty-one years?
"We're here because we're here because
we're here because we're here . . ."
we sang through ankle depths of dust
that hugged us as we marched,
and in our ordinariness that was enough,
even if there was, under the skin,
something we never
could have said,
and never needed to have said.
That we did it said the things it would
have embarrassed us
to say aloud.
Only one of us did try to say something,
the uncle who had stayed in the army

                                for twenty years,
and he wrote,
        "My youngest son who died of cancer when almost
three years old is buried in the National Cemetery in
Fort Bliss, Texas, among many young comrades. Both my other
sons were wounded in Viet Nam, the younger severely,
almost unto death. I neither encouraged nor discouraged
their joining the Armed Forces. I was proud on both occasions
for different reasons. Eldest son voluntarily joined the
Navy, and I was proud. Younger son vowed he would never
volunteer nor serve if called, and I was proud. He volunteered
for the draft after his closest friend was killed-in-action,
and I was both saddened and proud. Each and all of these
'prides' were difficult to accept for reasons that I believe
to be obvious."

                        It was only our ordinariness
                that gave any possible meaning
                                to those sixty-one years of service.

V

The death notices
        came drifting like small, firey embers
you couldn't close the door against,
                and they hung in the air
        with their burning persistence
    until the heart blazed up.
and the ticking of clocks
                was a low cracking of flames
                as you sat with hands propped
on a table and listened
                        to the roaring of the fire
within that was consuming you.
                On the radios, on the mantelpieces
        sat the photos in the stiff frames
                and the flames seemed to spread
over the flimsy sheen of glass
                that held them fixed there
        on their littered shelf.
I saw the photos in the newspapers,
        the faces of the ones who had died—

the eyes nervously staring, their
uniform hats on, mouths set,
as if the reality were only the sentences
in the newspaper articles,
as if it wasn't even death,
only a different kind of event
that the article was expected to explain.
The photos on the other pages,
of the bodies torn to bloodied rags,
never had any names,
It couldn't have been those bodies
that were the faces in the notices,
whose expression, if they had any
expression at all,
was only embarrassed surprise.

And I saw—
but how could I see? When I couldn't even
understand what was happening to them?—
but I saw the sudden sagging of faces
of women who had been wives, mothers,
sisters, I saw the stiff walk of men
who had been fathers, and who had to keep—somehow—
walking,
and there was a kind of still cry
that was stifled in the heart,
where the small fires
had singed it.
If the photographs had been printed together,
the headline reading,
"Private Ernie Hansen, son of
Mr. and Mrs. Paul Hansen, 1237 Westlake Drive,
of this city, seen shortly after his death
in combat last Thursday afternoon, January 16,"
and the picture one of a
torn, bleeding body instead of the
formal, embarrassed portrait,
would someone have said then,
no,
this is too much, no,
we can't bear it.

What did we say? What did they say?

    "God,"
some said,
    "God, take and keep,
this, thy servant ..."
    "God,"
some said,
    "In thy infinite mercy,
help us to understand ..."
    "God,"
some said.

And others said,
    "No, I can't believe,
I can't accept . . ."
and others said,
    "I can't believe,
I can't forgive . . ."
     And they stayed alone,
       and they stared into the emptiness
         until the silence deafened them.

        And I understood so little,
standing in the hallways in front of
     dim mirrors, with their sagging uniforms
        draped over my thin shoulders,
listening to their noisy shrill of laughter,
     and some of them died,
     whose caps I had tried on,
        and some of them
came up the stairs again,
      and their uniforms were stuffed into
      boxes to put in the back of
the closet, and we met again
     and their faces lost their lined sunburn,
       and we came to know each other,
     but of those who died,
       I knew so little.

WILLIAM STAFFORD
At the Grave of My Brother: Bomber Pilot

Tantalized by wind, this flag that flies
to mark your grave discourages those nearby
graves, and all still marching this hillside chanting,
    "Heroes, thanks. Goodby."

If a visitor may quiz a marble sentiment,
was this tombstone quarried in that country
where you slew thousands likewise honored
    of the enemy?

Reluctant hero, drafted again each Fourth
of July, I'll bow and remember you. Who
shall we follow next? Who shall we kill
    next time?

CORRINNE HALES
Consummation

Traveling at about 350 m.p.h., three Italian jets slammed together two hundred feet
above the main runway of Ramstein U.S. Air Base in West Germany and plunged into
thousands of spectators below, spewing fire and airplane parts over tents, cars, barbe-
cue grills—and people. It was the worst air show accident in history.

For K.J.S. (1947–1988)

After school the day John Kennedy died,
We drove your red Chevy fast
And terrified to the Lake, where we held on tight

Until midnight, and after. I remember screeching
Seagulls, the slight sting of salt water air, your face
In the last light, and how even the polished cherrywood

Knob on the stick shift seemed to shine softly
In dash-glow as we began slowly to make ourselves
Whole again by simple touch.

From that day on, the world got steadily colder
And we learned to trust only the heat and power
Of our own joined bodies, the clean, rhythmic energy

We discovered night after night wrapped
In the loose patchwork quilt you carried against whatever
Bad news was on its way.

I learned by heart the precise geography
Of your sixteen-year-old chest, and my fingers
Memorized the smooth hollow near your throat.

After all these years, you call out of nowhere,
Tell me you're in California and want us
To get together before you leave.

So, halfway to the coast one afternoon, I find myself
Waiting anxiously at a roadside diner. You've rejoined
The army, but look good anyway, and we fall quickly

Into our old argument—the circumstance
That has squeezed our lives
Into their current ragged shapes.

But that was last year—before I saw
News footage of the horrible Italian jets, bursting
Into flaming chunks, exploding into crowds

Caught in mid-cheer, and into a medivac helicopter fueled
And waiting on the sidelines. You'd think a person
Would know if a loved one were involved

In one of these documented tragedies
That show up so persistently on t.v.,
But I'd watched the thing replaying dozens of times

Before someone called to tell me you were there.
During the two weeks it has taken you
To die in the burn unit of a Texas military hospital,

Time has become strangely twisted. I'm speaking to you now
As if you were alive. I keep watching this film of fire
Crashing down on an American

Air base in Germany. People keep calling
With grim details—how long you were conscious, the extent
Of your burns, your last words

To your family, the exact condition
Of your beautiful skin.
At fifteen, I believed we'd always be

In love; we were the chosen ones
Who'd make it out
Of our sorry neighborhood, have a life

In the suburbs, eat steak and shrimp, go to work
Every day in clean, happy offices
Like all those pretty people in John F. Kennedy's

Television America. It was the space age
And we were the greatest, greenest country in the world
And the future smelled so sweet

It almost didn't matter that your mother had lost
Another tired job, that my house had no heat and smelled
Soggy with boiled cabbage, dirty diapers and too many

Runny-nosed kids. By then, my crazy father
And his hopeless anger had been taken away
For good. I had a job cleaning motel rooms, and you—

You had a car. For that brief adolescent moment
It really looked like America
Was going to let us in.

But the future was already rising
Across the eastern sky, prying at us
With its bloodstained fingers, and before either of us

Understood why, you'd already answered
The nation's first chilling knock
At our neighborhood's door. I am talking

To a dead man. In this photo, you are holding
A beautiful Vietnamese child on your lap. *I wish*
I could bring her home, your letter said. *She has no life*

Here anymore. Why not? I wrote back. Angry
for answers, I had only questions. Who killed her family
Anyway? What are you doing there, so far from home

And working for everything I hate?
Had you forgotten the photographs—the burning
Buddhist monks, so brilliantly consumed

By their own human desire? Their unswerving faith
In the good public dream? They made
No compromises. Hadn't we seen the same pictures?

Someone was trying to change the subject.
By 1966, a nervous citizen had already shot
A .22 caliber hole through my brother's leg

For stealing gasoline, I was pregnant, and lying my way
Through high school, working nights pressure cooking
Chicken in hot grease, and watching

Good mothers and ministers feed
The best of our young bodies
Methodically into the hungry national machine

Grinding out democracy, democracy,
Democracy. Recruiters cruised
The schools like pimps, with their spit-

Shined rhetoric, draft threats, powerful
Promises. You could smell smoke
On any American street. The attempt to settle

Our differences is still, I suppose,
Going on. Here at this diner, over coffee
And hot cherry pie, you try again to convince me

I should go to church. You tell me God and the army
Have given you the life we dreamed about
As kids. I tell you I've given myself

That life: I have good work, a house, furniture,
A family almost grown. It looks like
Both of us have made it.

But for some reason—as if we are survivors
Of some cosmic extermination plot—
We each feel chronically compelled

To convince the other of the rightness
Of our separate escapes. You keep playing
With the salt shaker, making neat white lines

With your fingers that scatter
Across the table as we talk. I think about the specific
Slow heat generated by the joining of hands

And the distinct hot sting of a slap. I want to touch
Your face. Vietnam was nearly half our lives
Ago, and you look forward to peacetime

Assignment in Germany. Your family
Will be with you, and you'll be flying
Some kind of helicopter ambulance

For the army. This is the dream
You say you've lived for. I wonder if it's worth it
To sell yourself for any middle-aged American dream.

What choice do we have? You ask me.
What choice did we ever have?
What did the likes of us have to offer

Except our own bodies?
I guess it's true. You sold your body to God, LBJ
And Richard Nixon; I sold mine to a man

With a job, and have had to steal what was left of it
Back. You and I spent the entire summer
You returned arguing

These things while my husband worked
The mines outside Salt Lake City. Everything was
Out of place. You'd become the enemy

I'd been working against—and I had to make you see it
My way. We planted a garden—
Spinach, tomatoes, peppers, peas. You helped me

Bake bread, we smoked a little, we talked, we touched,
We took my daughter to the park. We tried hard
To help each other heal.

But the deep invisible seam
That once had joined us so securely
At the edges of our skin had pulled apart

In the strain of making choices
We used to imagine we were free
To make. How did we end up

In these opposite camps?
The heroic immolation of Buddhist monks had given way
In *Life Magazine* to new photos of flaming

Napalmed children running frantically away
From whatever public passion
They were being called upon to fuel.

What better life had been promised them
By the cool national knock at their village door?
You said I didn't understand.

But hadn't you and I decided to climb
Together, pulling the others with us
Out of the grim pit of our beginnings? What happened

To that strong singular will? That spring,
At the city zoo, we watched a deer give birth. The spindly
Awkward thing dropped almost accidentally

To the ground, squirmed desperately for a few hard minutes,
The mother licking it for all she was worth
Until finally the legs took hold, and a new creature

Found the only way to make its life.
You began, that summer
To go back to church. It had some connection

To the war—you said you had to believe in
God's blessing a country that promised to pay you back
With a regular job, college education, and medical care

For the asking. I watch the foreign sheets of fire
Rain down on what has turned out to be
Your middle-aged body. Two weeks

And many far away phone calls later,
I sit in my California garden, staring out
At the bluest sky, still scared and angry

That we've been pitted so squarely
Against each other all these years. A mockingbird
Chases a squirrel loudly out of the crepe myrtle

Onto a sagging power line. The cat purrs,
Rubs its satisfied back
Against my ankle, and I'm suddenly sure

We should've left that reunion diner last year
Together, driven all the way
To the coast, tried one more time to touch

Our way back to the pure physical
Strength of a common purpose. But both of us
Were too far gone by then, and life

Is a very expensive commodity. We hugged
A clumsy goodbye at our separate cars, and I sped back
Across the valley to my good life, knowing

That most of the others we grew up with
Were already dead or living at the bottom, still
Balanced on the lowest rung

Of some narrow imaginary ladder
Leading up to this national dream, where the climb
Turns out to be nothing

But a lonely deal you have to make
With a world you can't trust for anything
Except that someone will come someday to collect.

PAMALA KAROL [LA LOCA]
War

Red Sun
over Echo Park
orbiting
an unheard-of botany
of disfigured statues
sprung never far from
the twig.
Underneath this fig leaf
my mother became an atheist.

A persimmon's throw from Black Monday
were the clack of the trolleys
the stomp of the Lindy
the crackle of zootsuiters spindling reefers
the pixilated palms
the plump Temple
& you
made in the image of
banana curls, leviathan dimples
& empires hemmed at the Veneris.
You
in the baked brick ice box
the one room
where you lived your whole life
with delivered milk
where your mother rose at 5 A.M.
and your father was a handyman.
How did you touch yourself
I wonder
in a room
crowded with
their separation
and your dream
of aquatic ballet?

You all kept your volcanos quiet
during the blackout
while you lay still

waiting for the hum
of the kamikazes.

Outside
the patriotic wore their designations:
I Am Chinese.

Inside
the world was made safe
for your mother
to work long hours
as a janitor in the annihilation industry.
She wore duck coveralls.

Your father,
too old to be conscripted,
conscripted you.
He did you up in his contumely;
his belittlement of you
in the one dress you owned
and how stupid you were.
His round eyes grew rounder
at the sight of his spitting image
biting her fingernails
in the ditch of Eden.
And you said to him,
"Am I going to be blown up?"

Down swept the sky with talons
with its jowls, with its beard
with its red bull's eye
and its impregnating pupil:
"Let me show you what a man is!"
Echo Park fell
and a scientist has the right
to insert his tongue
into the mouth of any child.
Hands for blades;
fingers: incisors;
he strapped you,
in the extinction position,
to his table of ablation.
It was over in a minute.

Your swimming pool in pieces in the sky.
Your obedience to the
hydrophobe who got you
in the kitchen.
He made legs out of you.
The bomb,
with the mousetrap in its womb,
delivered.
Your backstroke in the Milky Way,
Your life jacket of morbidity,
Your nipples,
all puerile and all thrumbs:
a fresh white flag
hung in the middle of the wish for death.
"Good Morning, Mr. & Mrs. America.
This morning, at 8:15 A.M.,
In Hiroshima, an industrial city
Fifteen hundred miles southwest of Tokyo
140,000
Japanese . . . Japanese . . . Japanese . . . Japanese"

Your mother came home, fatigued.
She pulled off her boots
and tied on an apron.
A pin dropped.
And you could hear
Krakatoa
as far away as
the sun.

ALLEN GINSBERG
How to Make a March/Spectacle

If imaginative, pragmatic, fun, gay, happy, *secure* Propaganda is issued
    to mass media in advance (and pragmatic leaflets handed out days
    in advance giving marchers instructions
The parade can be made into an exemplary spectacle on how to handle
    situations of anxiety and fear/threat
(such as Spectre of Hells Angels or Spectre of Communism)

To manifest by concrete example, namely the parade itself, how to change war psychology and surpass, go over, the habit- image-reaction of fear/violence.

That is, the parade can embody an example of peaceable health which is the reverse of fighting back blindly.

Announce in advance it is a safe march, bring your grandmother and babies, bring your family and friends. Open declarations, "We aren't coming out to fight and we simply will not fight."

We have to use our *imagination*. A spectacle can be made, an unmistakable statement OUTSIDE the war psychology which is leading nowhere. Such statement would be heard round the world with relief.

The following suggestions manifest or embody what I believe to be the conscious psychology of latent understanding of the majority of the youth and many elders who come out to march.

And once clearly enunciated by the leaders of the march will be clearly understood and acted upon by them. Necessary to TRUST the communal sanity of the marchers who already demonstrated that community when they first SAT DOWN.

Needed: an example of health which will paralyse the Angels and also manifest itself thru mass media reportage.

N.B. A negative psychology, of becoming scared by threats, adrenalin running in neck, uprush of blood to head, blind resentment, self-righteousness, fear, anger and active return of violence is exactly what the Angels "power structure" press and fuzz THRIVE ON
> what the young people who come march don't want and are dragged by
> what will decrease the number who come and discourage the great many on the fence who wd come to a good scene.

THE FOLLOWING are specific suggestions for organizing march and turning marchers on to their roles in the Demonstration.

• 1. Masses of flowers — a visual spectacle — especially concentrated in the front lines. Can be used to set up barricades, to present to Hells Angels, Police, politicians, and press & spectators whenever needed or at parade's end. Masses of marchers can be asked to bring their own flowers. Front lines shd. be organized & provided with flowers in advance.

• 2. Front lines should be the psychologically less vulnerable groups, The Women for Peace or any other respectable organization, perhaps a line of poets and artists, mothers, families, professors. This shd be announced (publicized in advance).

• 3. Marchers should bring CROSSES, to be held up in front in case of violence; like in the movies dealing with Dracula. (This for those who use crosses or Jewish Stars.)

• 4. Marchers who use American Flags should bring those: at least one front row of Marican flags and myriads in the spectacle.

• 5. Marchers should bring Harmonicas, flutes, recorders, guitars, banjos & violins. (Those who don't use crosses or flags) Bongoes and tambourines.

• 6. Marchers should bring certain children's Toys (not firecrackers or balloons which cause noise hysteria) which can be used for distracting attackers: such as sparklers, toy rubber swords, especially the little whirling carbon wheels which make red-white-blue sparkles. Toy soldiers.

• 7. In case of heavy anxiety, cónfusion or struggle in isolated spots marchers could be led in
    Sit Down
    Mass Calisthenics

• 8. In case of threat of attack marchers could intone en masse the following mantras
    The Lord's Prayer
    Three Blind Mice (*sung*)
    OM (AUM) *long breath in unison*
    Star Spangled Banner
    Mary Had a Little Lamb (*spoken in unison*)

• 9. More interesting Zen/Spectacle SIGNS
    As in Oakland so in Vietnam
    Everybody's Made of Meat
    Nobody Wants to Get Hurt—Us or Them

> Everybody's Wrong including U. S.
> Hells Angels   Vietcong   Birch Society
>
> <small>DON'T FLIP</small>
> We Love You Too

• 10. Candy bars carried by marchers to offer Hells Angels and Police.

• 11. Marchers encouraged to carry copies of the Constitution if they have them; or can buy them.

• 12. Little paper halos to offer angels, police and spectators & patriots.

• 13. A row of Marchers with white flags, & many white flags in mass.

• 14. Those who have movie cameras bring them and take pictures of spectacle or any action. (To combine for documentary film which could be used in court in case of legal hassels later, and also to circulate for propaganda and profits.) Monitors who can shd have cameras.

OTHER MORE GRANDIOSE POSSIBILITIES.

• 15. Corps of student newsmen to interview newsmen, propagandize & soften & charm TV crews etc.

• 16. Small floats or replicas in front:
> Christ with sacred heart & cross   *(invite church groups to prepare)*
>
> Buddha in Meditation   *(invite Zen people to come march & meditate on floats)*
>
> Geo Washington, Lincoln, Whitman etc.   *(float or living masquerade)*
>
> Thoreau behind bars   *(float)*
>
> Hell's Angles Float—With Halos, happy, praying   *(no ugly provocative caricature)*
>
> Birch Society Float   *(Old ladies in tennis sneakers)*
>
> Dixieland Band Foat dressed as Hitler Stalin Mussolini Napolean & Caesar   *(See Universal Soldier song)*

• 17.   At first sign of Disturbance, P.A. Systems swing into vast sound *I Wanna Hold Your Hand* and marchers instructed to dance (If not doing calisthenics or Lord's Prayer). (These could be schematized as strategy 1, 2, 3, etc for diverting crowd and angels from Violence.)

• 18.   The Mime Troupe in costume a block down the march, walking doing pantomime.

• 19.   Sound trucks with Bay Area Rock & Roll Bands every two blocks, Jefferson Airplanes, Charlatans, etc. (These bands have their own sound systems) This scheme to pick up on the universal Youth rockroll protest of Dylan, Eve of Destruction, Universal Soldier, etc. & concretize all that consciousness in the parade.

• 20.   Front (or toward front)—Toy army in costume, Civil War or Rev War or WW I uniforms and signs
NO MORE
LEAVE ME ALONE

AMY CLAMPITT
The Dahlia Gardens

There are places no history can reach. —Norman Mailer, *Armies of the Night*

Outside the river entrance, between the Potomac
and the curbed flowerbeds, a man walks up and down,
has been walking this last half hour. November leaves
skip in the wind or are lifted, unresisting,
to mesh with the spent residue of dahlias'
late-summer blood and flame, leached marigolds,
knives of gladioli flailed to ribbons:
parts of a system that seems, on the face of it,
to be all waste, entropy, dismemberment;
but which perhaps, given time enough, will prove
to have refused nothing tangible,
                              enjambed
without audible clash, with no more than a whiplash
incident, to its counterpart, a system
shod in concrete, cushioned in butyl, riding
chariots of thermodynamics, adept with the unrandom,

the calculus of lifting and carrying, with vectors,
clocks, chronicles, calibrations.
                                    File clerks
debouch into the dusk—it is rush hour; headlights
thicken, a viscous chain along the Potomac—
from concentric corridors, five sides
within five sides, grove leading on to grove
lit by autonomous purrings, daylight
on demand, dense with the pristine,
the dead-white foliage of those archives
that define and redefine with such precision,
such subtleties of exactitude, that only
the honed mind's secret eye can verify
or vouch for its existence, how the random
is to be overcome, the unwelcome
forestalled, the arcane calamity
at once refused, delineated and dwelt on. Where,
as here, true Precaution, Accumulation
and Magnitude obtain, such levitations
and such malignities have come, with time,
to seem entirely natural—this congeries
being unquestionably the largest
office building in Christendom.
                                    The man alone
between blackened flowerbeds and the blackening
Potomac moves with care, as though balanced
astride the whiplash between system and system—
wearing an overcoat, hatless, thinning-haired,
a man of seemingly mild demeanor
who might have been a file clerk
were it not for his habit of writing down
notes to himself on odd scraps of paper,
old bills, the backs of envelopes, or in a notebook
he generally forgets to bring with him,
and were it not for the wine jug
he carries (the guard outside the river entrance,
as he pauses, has observed it, momentarily puzzled)
cradled close against his overcoat.
                                    By now file clerks,
secretaries, minor and major bureaucrats, emerging
massively through the several ports of egress,
along the ramps, past the walled flowerbeds,
which the lubrications and abrasions of routine,

the multiple claims of a vigilant anxiety,
the need for fine tuning, for continual
readjustment of expectation, have rendered
largely negligible, flow around him.
He moves against the flux, toward the gardens.
Around him, leaves skip in the wind
like a heartbeat, like a skipped
heartbeat

> *if I were a dead leaf*
> *thou mightest bear*

He shivers,
cradling the wine jug, his heart beating strangely;
his mind fills up with darkness

> overland, the inching caravans
> the blacked-out troop trains
> convoys through ruined villages
> along the Mekong

merging
with the hydrocarbon-dark, headlight-inflamed Potomac

the little lights   the candles
flickering on Christmas eve
the one light left burning
in a front hallway   kerosene-
lit windows in the pitch dark
of back-country roads

His mind
plunges like a derrick
into that pitch dark as he uncorks the wine jug
and with a quick gesture not unlike
a signing with the cross (but he is a Quaker)
begins the anointing of himself with its contents,
with the ostensible domestic Rhine wine
or chablis, which is not wine—which
in fact is gasoline.

> tallow, rushlight, whale oil, coal oil,
> gas jet: black fat of the Ur-tortoise
> siphoned from stone, a shale-tissued

carapace: hydrocarbon unearthed
and peeled away, process by process,
in stages not unlike the stages
of revolution, to a gaseous plume
that burns like a bush, a perpetual
dahlia of incandescence, midway
between Wilmington and Philadelphia
gaslight, and now these filamented
avenues, wastelands and windows
of illumination, gargoyles,
gasconades, buffooneries of neon,
stockpiled incendiary pineapples,
pomegranates of jellied gasoline
that run along the ground, that cling
in a blazing second skin
to the skins of children

Anointing the overcoat, and underneath it the pullover
with one elbow out, he sees, below the whiplash threshold,
darkness boil up, a vatful of sludge, a tar pit,
a motive force that is all noise: jet engines,
rush-hour aggressions, blast furnaces,
headline-grabbing self-importances

the urge to engineer events
compel a change of government,
a change of heart, a shift
in the wind's direction—lust
after mastery, manipulations
of the merely political

Hermaphrodite of pity and violence, the chambered
pistol and the sword-bearing archangel,
scapegoat and self-appointed avenger, contend,
embrace, are one. He strikes the match.
A tiger leap, a singing envelope goes up,
blue-wicked, a saffron overcoat of burning

in the forests of the night
make me thy lyre

Evolving
out of passionless dismemberment,
a nerveless parturition, green wheels'

meshed intercalibration with the sun

A random leaf, seized by the updraft, shrivels
unresisting, fragments of black ash
drift toward the dahlia gardens

    from dim tropisms of avoidance,
    articulated, node upon internode,
    into a scream, the unseen filament
    that never ends, that runs
    through all our chronicles

    a manifesto flowering like a dahlia
    into whole gardens of astonishment—
    the sumptuous crimson,
    heart's dark, the piebald
    saffron and scarlet riding
    the dahlia gardens of
    the lake of Xochimilco:

    Benares, marigold-garlanded
    suttee, the burning ghats
    alongside the Ganges: at
    the An Quang pagoda, saffron
    robes charring in fiery
    transparency, a bath of burning

Scraps of charred paper, another kind of foliage,
drift toward the dahlia gardens

                 a leaf
    thou mightest bear

                         The extravaganza
of a man afire having seized, tigerlike, the attention
it now holds with the tenacity of napalm, of the homebound
file clerks, secretaries, minor and major bureaucrats,
superimposing upon multiple adjustments,
the fine tuning of Precaution and Accumulation,
the demands of Magnitude, what the concentric
groves of those archives have no vocabulary
for dwelling on, the uniformed man of action,

in whom precaution and the unerring impulse
are one, springs forward to pound and pummel,
extinguishing the manifesto as decently as possible.

                                             Someone,

by now, has sent for an ambulance.

The headlights crawl, slowed by increasing density,
along the Potomac, along the diagonal thoroughfares,
along the freeways, toward Baltimore, toward Richmond,
toward Dulles and the municipal airport, the airborne
engines' alternating red
and green, a pause then again a red,
a green, a waking fantasy upborne
on a lagoon of hydrocarbon, as
the dahlia gardens ride the lake of Xochimilco.
While the voiceless processes of a system
that in the end perhaps will have
refused nothing tangible, continue neither
to own nor altogether to refuse the burning filament
that runs through all our chronicles, uniting
system with system into one terrible mandala,
the stripped hydrocarbon
burns like a bush, a gaseous plume
midway between Wilmington and Philadelphia.

An account of the self-immolation of a thirty-two-year-old Quaker, Norman Morrison, in front of the Pentagon in Washington appeared in *The New York Times* on November 3, 1965. Although his name has since been forgotten in the United States, in 1978 it was (according to an American visitor whose report I happened to hear) still remembered in Vietnam.

"Midway between Wilmington and Philadelphia": the refineries of Marcus Hook, Pennsylvania, with their perpetual gas flares, will be familiar to anyone who has traveled through the region via Amtrak.

Charles Olson's observation that the first oil well had been drilled as recently as 1859 was what dramatized for me the transitoriness of an entire culture founded on the use of petroleum: people to whom I report this fact are almost invariably startled, as though it could not possibly be true.

JOHN BALABAN
Words for My Daughter

About eight of us were nailing up forts
in the mulberry grove behind Reds's house
when his mother started screeching and
all of us froze except Reds — fourteen, huge
as a hippo — who sprang out of the tree so fast
the branch nearly bobbed me off. So fast,
he hit the ground running, hammer in hand,
and seconds after he got in the house
we heard thumps like someone beating a tire
off a rim   his dad's howls the screen door
banging open   Saw   Reds barreling out
through the tall weeds towards the highway
the father stumbling after his fat son
who never looked back across the thick swale
of teazel and black-eyed susans until it was safe
to yell fuck you at the skinny drunk
stamping around barefoot and holding his ribs.

Another time, the Connelly kid came home to find
his alcoholic mother getting raped by the milkman.
Bobby broke a milkbottle and jabbed the guy
humping on his mom. I think it really happened
because none of us would loosely mention that
wraith of a woman who slippered around her house
and never talked to anyone, not even her kids.
Once a girl ran past my porch
with a dart in her back, her open mouth
pumping like a guppy's, her eyes wild.
Later that summer, or maybe the next,
the kids hung her brother from an oak.
Before they hoisted him, yowling and heavy
on the clothesline, they made him claw the creekbank
and eat worms. I don't know why his neck didn't snap.

Reds had another nickname you couldn't say
or he'd beat you up: "Honeybun."
His dad called him that when Reds was little.

*

So, these were my playmates. I love them still
for their justice and valor and desperate loves
twisted in shapes of hammer and shard.
I want you to know about their pain
and about the pain they could loose on others.
If you're reading this, I hope you will think,
Well, my Dad had it rough as a kid, so what?
If you're reading this, you can read the news
and you know that children suffer worse.

*

Worse for me is a cloud of memories
still drifting off the South China Sea,
like the 9-year-old boy, naked and lacerated,
thrashing in his pee on a steel operating table
and yelling, *"Dau. Dau,"* while I, trying to translate
in the mayhem of Tet for surgeons who didn't know
who this boy was or what happened to him, kept asking
"Where? Where's the pain?" until a surgeon
said "Forget it. His ears are blown."

*

I remember your first Hallowe'en
when I held you on my chest and rocked you,
so small your toes didn't touch my lap
as I smelled your fragrant peony head
and cried because I was so happy and because
I heard, in no metaphorical way, the awful chorus
of Soeur Anicet's orphans writhing in their cribs.
Then the doorbell rang and a tiny Green Beret
was saying trick-or-treat and I thought *oh oh*
but remembered it was Hallowe'en and where I was.
I smiled at the evil midget, his map-light and night
paint, his toy knife for slitting throats, said
"How ya doin', soldier?" and, still holding you asleep
in my arms, gave him a Mars Bar. To his father
waiting outside in fatigues I hissed, "You shit,"
and saw us, child, in a pose I know too well.

I want you to know the worst and be free from it.
I want you to know the worst and still find good.

Day by day, as you play nearby or laugh
with the ladies at Peoples Bank as we go around town
and I find myself beaming like a fool,
I suspect I am here less for your protection
than you are here for mine, as if you were sent
to call me back into our helpless tribe.

W. D. EHRHART

Letter to the Survivors

To any who find this,
understand:

year by year, we could see it
approaching—the tensions
mounting, the missiles
mounting, the bombers
rising, the submarines slipping
down their long thin launch-ramp rails,
the warheads, and multiple warheads.
We knew it,
but we were afraid.
We were ordinary people, only
the work-a-day Marys and Joes.
Our leaders insisted
they were striving for peace.
What could we do
but believe them?
We had only our one vote each,
only our small voices;
and it was a crime to refuse
to serve, and a crime
to refuse to pay.
We did not want to lose our friends;
we did not want to lose our jobs;
we did not want to lose our homes—

and we didn't really believe
it could happen.

Guerrilla War

It's practically impossible
to tell civilians
from the Vietcong.

Nobody wears uniforms.
They all talk
the same language,
(and you couldn't understand them
even if they didn't).

They tape grenades
inside their clothes,
and carry satchel charges
in their market baskets.

Even their women fight;
and young boys,
and girls.

It's practically impossible
to tell civilians
from the Vietcong;

after a while,
you quit trying.

The One That Died

You bet we'll soon forget the one that died;
he isn't welcome any more.
He could too easily take our place
for us to think about him
any longer than it takes
to sort his personal effects:
        a pack of letters,
        cigarettes,
        photos and a wallet.
We'll keep the cigarettes;

divide them up among us.
His parents have no use for them,
and cigarettes are hard to get.

Coming Home

San Francisco airport—

no more corpsemen stuffing ruptured chests
with cotton balls and not enough heat tabs
to eat a decent meal.

I asked some girl to sit
and have a coke with me.
She thought I was crazy;
I thought she was going to call a cop.

I bought a ticket for Philadelphia.
At the loading gate, they told me:
"Thank you for flying TWA;
we hope you will enjoy your flight."

No brass bands;
no flags,
no girls,
no cameramen.

Only a small boy who asked me
what the ribbons on my jacket meant.

Imagine

The conversation turned to Vietnam.
He'd been there, and they asked him
what it had been like:
had he been in battle?
Had he ever been afraid?

Patiently, he tried to answer
questions he had tried to answer
many times before.

They listened, and they strained
to visualize the words:
newsreels and photographs, books
and Wilfred Owen tumbled
through their minds.
Pulses quickened.

They didn't notice, as he talked,
his eyes, as he talked,
his eyes began to focus
through the wall, at nothing,
or at something inside.

When he finished speaking,
someone asked him:
had he ever killed?

BRUCE WEIGL

Song of Napalm

for my wife

After the storm, after the rain stopped pounding,
We stood in the doorway watching horses
Walk off lazily across the pasture's hill.
We stared through the black screen,
Our vision altered by the distance
So I thought I saw a mist
Kicked up around their hooves when they faded
Like cut-out horses
Away from us.
The grass was never more blue in that light, more
Scarlet; beyond the pasture
Trees scraped their voices into the wind, branches
Crisscrossed the sky like barbed wire
But you said they were only branches.

Okay. The storm stopped pounding.
I am trying to say this straight: for once
I was sane enough to pause and breathe
Outside my wild plans and after the hard rain

I turned my back on the old curses. I believed
They swung finally away from me . . .

But still the branches are wire
And thunder is the pounding mortar,
Still I close my eyes and see the girl
Running from her village, napalm
Stuck to her dress like jelly,
Her hands reaching for the no one
Who waits in waves of heat before her.

So I can keep on living,
So I can stay here beside you,
I try to imagine she runs down the road and wings
Beat inside her until she rises
Above the stinking jungle and her pain
Eases, and your pain, and mine.

But the lie swings back again.
The lie works only as long as it takes to speak
And the girl runs only as far
As the napalm allows
Until her burning tendons and crackling
Muscles draw her up
Into that final position
Burning bodies so perfectly assume. Nothing
Can change that: she is burned behind my eyes
And not your good love and not the rain-swept air
And not the jungle-green
Pasture unfolding before us can deny it.

ROBERT WRIGLEY
Shrapnel

"Shrapnel," he says to me, "seems wrong,"
for the filament of steel that tore his spine
is nothing like what the word suggests.
Tiny, elegant, almost blunt,

it is his amulet in a film can,
each day taken out and caressed,
worn smooth and shiny as a bearing.

I have come to know him
through our morning walks, mine afoot,
his in a wheelchair with a shepherd dog
called Hue. Just as you probably suspect
he wears an army field jacket and a beard.
With an old racket he hammers a tennis ball
half a block for his dog to chase.

For a year now it is I
who have hit the ball for Hue,
while his master visits the naturopath
for herbal packs and high colonics,
his legs, he swears, more alive than ever,
shimmering in his lap with cold fire,
a sweet and unlocalized tingling.

He has asked me, politely, almost shyly,
for poems, and I give them to him—
Wilfred Owen and Weigl—
and he reads them on the spot,
slowly and carefully, like love letters
or contracts. Always, when he is finished,
he murmurs and folds them away in a pocket.

Sometimes we talk about the weather
or women, and then I have to leave
for school, so we wave and go our opposite ways,
he with his dog who loves him
and I with my messages of art
and the word. From the back porch
of his little house he watches

high school boys batter themselves silly
on the practice football field,
and I enter this new brick building,
stiflingly hot, ragged with conversations,
and stride to the front of the room
and survey the young faces, already bored,
and find, for some reason, I cannot speak.

I don't blame them, you know.
It must look those mornings
as though I've lost my mind, or my way.
I want to tell them sometimes I died
in the war I refused to go near.
Truly, I am ashamed
for my life, my lies, my legs.

Today, we will speak of Robert Frost,
his ambitions, his perfections.
They have read a few poems
and I have a film to show,
but as always I begin with a word,
sometimes plucked from the blustery fall air
for no good reason but the mind

and its hard affiliations with the world.
I am quite entertaining some days,
going on about the harsh aestetics of *phlegm*
or the mouthy succulence of *undulate.*
They know what's coming. I walk
back and forth, back and forth,
until the right word comes, and changes nothing.

GEORGE EVANS
from Under the World

ESCAPED EXOTICS

Baby curls sucking a sweater heap,
urban Madonna scene late century 20,
mouthing wool on a breast mountain,
jerking,
clamped to mother flesh,
with the tit slid out of range,
raisin-like anyway.

Air rush. Bay light. Money jungle.
Cardboard and sacks slow twist and kick,
wake and yawn with traffic in graffiti blight,

                       spray paint glyphs on underpass,
                         waking up below the troughs
                 pouring lucky ones workward or home.

•

                Long saxual wail rips
                from their fire barrels,
            heat blurred figure circled,
        one wheezing a sax through rail
                 and bus roar
             morning stink and noise

•

This one has seen it all, his
eye opening in a blanket hole,
hears a crash without moving.

<u>Up, Get up!</u>,foot kicks.
He tries, falls back in trance, another crash,
worms out, sniffs oxide, rusting track,
then there's the scene beyond the chainlink
warped, turned up for exits:
two cars crushed like paper, origami giants.

The drivers scream throwing their heads.

In shaving cream, rollers, and whispers,
the underpass crowd packs carts,
strikes tents, undoes the night.

He gets up and walks wrapped in his blanket
through steam twist over sewer lids.

<u>Nicely dramatic, nice, nice, nice, like the evening news</u>
the one called Pinkeye says, <u>very nice, good effect.</u>

A loose one, strange one. Everything <u>nice</u>,everything
part of a stage. Chanting <u>Pinkeye Pinkeye Pinkeye Poink</u>,
lifting foot to rub his knee, then perch. Flamingo scarf.

Eye in the blanket, Love, Charles Love, slides up,
shifting from sleep array and dishevel scratch.
Drivers take numbers, explain, scream.
He watches Pinkeye fidget, hair twisted sticking out,
ginseng roots, in overcoat, cherubic face with cynical eyes,

white circles rubbed around the sockets, who
losing interest struts akimbo near the wreck,
begins:

Friends, subjects, and projects, I'm recovering from everything
        but I'll be fine   god protects Emperors by driving them mad
there's a certain form of perfection in that   that is of course
        you know   what Medusa is all about   all a question
of looking the mortal world in its eyes   haha haha haha   not
just looking but   [waves a finger]   **REALLY**   looking
at this nest of snakes   steady boys steady   staring until until
until you're   **STONE FUCKING STONE**   Ha!   unable to act upon
        E-E-E-E-E-Emotions

and but   the tissues of love the tissues
and but   the tissues of fate
and but   coincide with the collapsing west
and but   ern world and bring me
and but   to conclude
and but   everything should be as it is
and but   in a Reynolds painting at least
and but   with clouds like walls of cities and sun
                        like a living thing, delightful, delightful
                    is the way it should be
across my minions and minions of minions my dears

He hates these types.
Too predictable
Everyone is looking
with eyes some other place,
but not him not Love

                        (Charles Love, Charlie Love, Chuckie Love,
                        Sergeant Love, Mr. Love, Crazy Love)

Rubbing fingerless gloves together
watching Pinkeye,
paying attention
to what moves in case it turns,
then wanders off.

WORDS IN THE UNDERPASS

I hid in fear

wing-crushed

born in the arms of an enemy with my mother
            strong enough
                        to break loose
                                    without flicker

            the shadow he cast

the dark swirl of purple blood rising around her eyes,

                                    mother's cane,

                                    her keeper—

            What was that, Love thought,
            what did that mean beyond
                rattle how could it
            mean, who are these people?

I'm not above the law, I am the law   wearing socks with toes
cut off for sleeves, and several shirts.

Who?

                Everything almost true but rootless,
                almost visible and exact but crazed.

Twenty years gone,
his body still traveling through it, in it,
humping the weight, shifted now to brain weight,
head of many pounds, who tried everything then failed,
who walks with his head falling off,
wished and shouted away as an irritation,
stinking of urine and evil and insect blood,
a nail driven in the face, footprint on the face,
snapped, unable to be unwilling to stay the same,
too obvious to be interesting or worth recovery,
too gone, too nothing, too much,
outside the realm of demand,
outside the realm of desire,
desire

                        [Too much, baby, too

194

A woman pushes her monkey-faced baby and shopping cart down-
town
        baby bouncing
    up and down having learned to stand wind
    whistling through cart ribs, combing streets, mother
    homicidal, hungry enough to eat the baby,
    grief welling, bouncing rattling

pushing ahead they proceed
hands spread
knots of paper
cans and bones
ahead

burst between cars

                         •

        A secret knowledge,
   possession of those without possessions,
    property of those without property,
   baby in hands of those without hands,
    visions for eyes tired by visions
                         •

It's not that he doesn't belong,
but that it's in his head.   That that's the state
of being non-being.   That that is common.   Non-being
is in the head, and a state of being common,
end 20th Century America unto infinity.
There are no cowboys.

        Everywhere from everywhere:

LOVE, YOU SUMBITCH,   *"All you borrow returns,"*
RUCKITY RICKETY LONG-COCKED FOOL,   *all you returns repeats,*
GIMME DIME!   *what you borrows returns,*
                              what you returns repeats,
                               borrow returns,
                                returns repeats,
                              repeated multiplies
                          return . . . "

Parson came to look at my garden
said: That ain't much, but
then again, you ain't either."

HAHAHA. Always did like
that particular religion.   [Gimme that, fool

                              Eyes float, hair shakes:
                              Now I'm gonna quotate Cus
                              D'Amato, he says, now its
                                let's see it's no it's um
                                he says ah yeah he says
                                'When you get hit, that's
                                when you gotta be calm,'
                                yeah, that's it, I'monna
                                  stretch out right chair
                                        and be calm

Who?

                                  [Hi, Sweetie pie!

VICTOR OF THE WOLVES

Walking out towards Market Street, he sees a tow truck jerking at the
wheelless van where Victor of the Wolves lives, the one who gives
everyone a color name: Blue Wolf, Black Wolf, Purple Wolf, White Wolf,
Gold Wolf, Silver Wolf, Yellow Wolf, Red Wolf, explaining he's organiz-
ing teams for a universal worldwide checker championship under the
freeways of America,
and who named Pinkeye, saying he'd run out of wolf colors, besides
which he didn't deserve to be a wolf because he drooled in his sleep,
and who stuck out his forearm to Love, naming him Green Wolf for his
camouflage fatigue pants and teeth, then shook his hand: This is my
promotion, he said, mine, leaving a sticky mark on Love's palm, who
stood shaking his head.

Now Victor was sitting against a wall near the grease shadow of the
van, belongings heaped beside him, head down and a thin line of drool
on his chin, talking: Fuck the fucking . . . a man without boots can't
suck bootstraps . . . dump the fuck they said, the fuck, dump the fuck,
a fuck dump, fuck a dump, I'm not a fuck dump, I'M A WOLF . . .
that's the black shadow of god, that stain, that van mark, plunging
hole, black vapors of sleep. There was another standing on an updraft
grate drying from a bath in the fountain, another a shaft of sunlight
pinning him stretched on a concrete pier, and an old Chinese woman,
her coats hung in a tree, slicing the air with Tai Chi.

VALENTINE'S DAY

The war is in his head today because of the crash
                                because of the smoke and sax at dawn
                        because of Pinkeye's insanity
                because of baby wail echo in the underpass
        and crevices in his white hands turned black
        because he lives in the streets and never gets home
                because he dreams in Vietnamese
        and the top of his head is torn by storm
    because he is too specific about his pain
        and his lips detach and fly through fanblades
    because his hands shake and he doesn't forget properly
because he was a soldier and junkie
            but can't remember which was worst,
                                    which eats his brain,
                                    which spits it out

    because starred nights pass over and through him in seconds
    because days have no time structure and he looks crazy
    because he is crazy   because he knows he's crazy
    because everyone keeps saying he's crazy he's crazy

The was is in his head today because it's cathartic
        because that's where it belongs
                    because that's what he's about
    because he held tiny white bones in his hand
            because those bones were attached to a baby
                because the baby looked at him, saw him
        because half the baby was missing
                    he was holding the baby when someone came up
                        from behind and cut it
                    because he's still holding the baby
                because he got a medal for holding the baby
because he hates himself for who came up behind
            to cut the baby in half which he was holding
                because he was holding the baby
                        because he's still holding the baby
        and because it is Wednesday,
yes, definitely because it is Wednesday

Revelation in the Mother Lode

I walk into the vineyard at night, into acres of cordoned vines
    against their stakes at pruning time, but see, stretching
    off through the fog, only cross marked graves.

How did it come to be that my generation would be stiff
    under hoarfrost, and that I should come across them
    twenty years after watching them die to remember and feel
    I've truly wasted my time, have left no mark upon the earth
    In their name, have left only the small craters of a boot
    sucking vineyard mud.

And is this guilt, or the product of being swept up
    in a time on human earth when few do more than raise
    the cause of their own names—and am I one, or is all this
    death just sloth which one pretends
    to work against the belly of
    but which in fact
    controls?

You who return to me as vines in the deep night under fog
    have come at a bad time, a time when the world is obsessed
    with rubbing you smooth, and its concentration
    on ceremony brings you to nothing.

Somewhere, mixed in with all the rest I'd meant to get to
    which is receding, is a day floating above jungle, flak
    exploding in small fists from the trees, rocking
    the chopper where I sit in shock and blood and urine
    staring into patchwork fields.

I stand behind bamboo shaking, thinking of Nguyet
    in a Saigon bar, worried how willingly we forget,
    bombs dropping like hair straight down   a shadow
    a black sheet   everything about us muscle   hot
    prick and resolve   and have no idea where I am
    but am everywhere   and she   wobbling on spiked heels
    around the bar stools and smoke has everything I cannot
    not the least of which is a reason
                    which makes her more beautiful
    than possible, but also quite a bit like the ragged edge
    of a ruined wall, and like the crisp brown bamboo leaves

dropping after terrible heat, dripping with an ache I love
which is more for youth than anything   certainly not war,
which also feels like dropping.

How tired I am of hearing about that war, which one should struggle
to keep the nightmare of, suffer from rather than forget.
I don't want to heal, and am sick of those who do.
Such things end in license.

Back here it turns out newspapers and monuments are taxidermy;
there is little retribution, little learning; what is lost
is forgotten; sometimes it gets so bad I'm not sure
I'm the one who lived . . . then come upon you in a field
—a one-time soldier with a trick knee, flagging humor,
monsoon debt—and find you enfolded by fog as if by spirits,
and become the visage of all that's been thrown from the world.

SAMUEL HAZO
War News Viewed in the Tropics

It seems like melodrama beamed
    from Mars: two Presidents like goats
    about to butt, marines in bunkers
    reading every letter's every word,
    tank captains squinting
    from their turrets "somewhere in Arabia."
Surrounded by mimosa, bougainvillea
    and palms, what sucks me back
    into this nausea for news?
                Remembering
    Seferis, I can say my country
    wounds me anywhere I go.
What's happening to us?
Is this how America's century
    ends?
               Why are we now
    so quick to kill however slowly
    and so slowly quick to sweat
    for peace?

For months we've acted
like the new crusaders, righteous
as Barbarossa and the British kings.
The true cross of our cause.
is true for everyone
because we say it is.
Not that we're trapped between
a tyrant and a sheikh with eighty
sons.
Not that we've bought
accomplices we call allies.
Not that
the sand will claim our camps
as surely as the years made wrecks
of Richard's castles near the coast.
Not that we've made a hoax
of history . . .
Meanwhile, old Moscow's
come apart like Rome, Constantinople
and Madrid.
Six-time-zones
wide, all Russia begs
like Ethiopia for bread.
The second
world's careening into bits.
Here in the third the islanders
respond to our new order
with their own.
They've started
hoarding kerosene.
They pray
unhopefully for peace.
They say
the worst is always unforeseen.

ROSMARIE WALDROP
from The Road is Everywhere
or Stop This Body

for Toni Warren

as if we could ignore
the consequences of
explosions fracture the present
warm exhaust
in our lungs would turn us
inside out of
gloves avoid words like
"war" needs subtler
poisons as if
conscious of ends and means
scream in every
nerve every breath every
grain of dust
to dust cancers over
the bloodstream
the bloodstream
the bloodstream
the bloodstream
the bloodstream

WILLIAM STAFFORD
Entering History

Remember the line in the sand?
You were there, on the telly, part of
the military. You didn't want to
give it but they took your money
for those lethal tanks and the bombs.

Minorities, they don't have a country
even if they vote: "Thanks, anyway,"
the majority says, and you are left there

staring at the sand and the line they drew,
calling it a challenge, calling it "ours."

Where was your money when the tanks
grumbled past? Which bombs did you buy
for the death rain that fell? Which year's
taxes put that fire to the town
where the screaming began?

WILLIAM HEYEN
The Truth

Aross Brockport Village, a blight of orange & yellow ribbons
meant to remember our half-million participants
in "Operation Desert Storm," those who put their lives on line
to protect our country, as our president says.
Darkening ribbons encircle trees, telephone poles,
mailboxes, porch rails—so I was understandably half bored
& half nuts with war & ugliness, so climbed to my roof
& tied a large black configuration of bow & ribbons
to my aerial. Up there, I saw how it divides the winter sky
with its alphabet of one emotional letter, a vowel. . . .

At first, no one noticed, but then a car turned around.
Later, a police cruiser slowed down, & then another.
A reporter stopped for that infamous photo that appeared in *Time*
& the first of a hundred interviews I declined,
& neighbors gathered. My phone kept ringing off the wall,
people yelling "bastard," & "traitor," & "get it the hell down,
or else." . . . Eventually, my best friend came to my door
& asked me why. I explained, "I can't explain." Others followed,
& insisted. "No comment," I said. "I don't want trouble,"
I said. "Read Hawthrone's 'The Minister's Black Veil.'"

I still like the way the black bow & ribbons flutter,
stark but suggestive of comic dark, serious, direct,
my own American allegiance & patriotic light.
Parson Hooper had his reasons, & half understood them,
but when he slept or spoke, his breath trembled the veil,
& even holy scripture seemed filtered by the terrible

transformation of black crepe into symbol. In the end,
not even his creator could commend the visionary parson
who espied the truth that separates & condemns.
Above my village, this beauty of black bow & ribbons.

HAYDEN CARRUTH

On Being Asked to Write a Poem
Against the War in Vietnam

Well I have and in fact
more than one and I'll
tell you this too

I wrote one against
Algeria that nightmare
and another against

Korea and another
against the one
I was in

and I don't remember
how many against
the three

when I was a boy
Abyssinia Spain and
Harlan County

and not one
breath was restored
to one

shattered throat
mans womans or childs
not one not

one
but death went on and on
never looking aside

except now and then like a child
with a furtive half-smile
to make sure I was noticing.

ROBERT CREELEY

Sonnets

for Keith and Rosmarie

Come round again the banal
belligerence almost a
flatulent echo of times
when still young the Sino
etc conflict starvation lists
of people without work or place
world so opaque and desperate
no one wanted even to
go outside to play even
with Harry Buddy who hit
me who I hit stood slugging
while they egged us on.

While ignorant armies clash
bash while on the motorway
traffic backed up while they
stand screaming at each other
while they have superior
armaments so wage just
war while it all provokes
excuses alternatives money
time wasted go tell it
on the town dump deadend
avoidance of all you might
have lived with once.

Someone told me to stand
up to whoever pushed me
down when talking walking
hand on friend's simple
pleasures thus abound when
one has fun with one

another said surrogate
God and planted lettuce
asparagus had horses cows
the farm down the road
the ground I grew up
on unwon unending.

I'd take all the learned
manner of rational un-
derstanding away leave
the table to stand on
its own legs and plates
to stick there the food
for who wants it the places
obvious and ample and
even in mind think it
could be other than an
argument a twisting
away tormented unless.

Me is finally unable having
as all seem to ended with
lost chances happily enough
missed the boat took them
all to hell on a whim
went over whatever precipice
but no luck just stupid
preoccupation common
fear of being overly hurt
by the brutal exigencies were
what pushed and pulled
me too to common cause.

So being old and wise and
unwanted left over from
teeth wearing hands wearing
clothes I put on take now
off and sleep or not or sit
this afternoon morning night
time's patterns look up at
stars overhead there what
do they mean but how useless
all violence how far away you
are from what you want.

Some people you just
know and recognize,
whether a need or fact,
a disposition at that
moment is placed,
you're home, a light
is in that simple
window forever— As if
people had otherwise always
to be introduced, told
you're ok— But here
you're home, so longed
for, so curiously
without question found.

PERMISSIONS

208

EVANS, GEORGE

"Revelation in the Mother Lode" first appeared in *Sudden Dreams* by George Evans, Coffee House Press, 1991. Reprinted by permission of the publisher. Copyright © 1991 by George Evans. "Under the World," Copyright © 1993 by George Evans. Reprinted by permission of the author.

EVERSON, WILLIAM

Reprinted from *The Masks of Drought,* "The Versailles Peace, 1936," Black Sparrow Press, 1980, by permission of the author.

GINSBERG, ALLEN

"Demonstration or Spectacle As Example, As Communication," Copyright © 1965 by Allen Ginsberg. Reprinted by permission of the author.

GIOVANNI, NIKKI

"To Be Black in America." Copyright © 1993 by Nikki Giovanni. Printed by permission of the author.

GOLDBARTH, ALBERT

"Of Ontology" appeared in *Carolina Quarterly.* Reprinted by permission of the author.

HALES, CORRINNE

"Consummation" appeared in *New England Review,* "Testimony" in *The Kenyon Review,* and "Sunday Morning" in *The Southern Review.* Reprinted by permission of the author.

HARJO, JOY

"For Anna Mae Pictou Aquash, Whose Spirit Is Present Here and in the Dappled Stars" by Joy Harjo, reprinted from *In Mad Love and War,* Wesleyan University Press, Copyright © 1990 by Joy Harjo, Wesleyan University Press by permission of the University Press of New England.

HAZO, SAMUEL

Reprinted from *The Past Won't Stay Behind You,* "War News Viewed in the Tropics," University of Arkansas Press, 1993. Reprinted by permission of the author.

Knight, Copyright © 1986 by Etheridge Knight. Reprinted by permission of the University of Pittsburgh Press.

KOMUNYAKAA, YUSEF

Reprinted from *Magic City*, "History Lessons," © 1992 by Yusef Komunyakaa, Wesleyan University Press by permission of the University Press of New England. "Modern Medea" and "New Amsterdam" by Yusef Komunyakaa, Copyright © 1993 by Yusef Komunyakaa. Printed by permission of the author.

KUMIN, MAXINE

"Leisure" and "Self-fulfilling Prophecy" from "Saga: Four Variations on the Sonnet" are reprinted from *Looking For Luck*, Poems by Maxine Kumin, by permission of the author and W. W. Norton & Company, Inc. Copyright © 1992 by Maxine Kumin.

LOGAN, WILLIAM

"Seduction of the Swimming Club," Copyright © 1994 by William Logan. Printed by permission of the author.

LOUIS, ADRIAN C.

"Sunset at Pine Ridge Agency," "Fullblood Girl on a Blue Horse" and "Pabst Blue Ribbon at Wounded Knee," Copyright © 1989, 1992, 1993, respectively, by Adrian C. Louis. Printed by permission of the author.

MADHUBUTI, HAKI R.

Reprinted from *Killing Memory, Seeking Ancestors*, "Aberrations," Lotus Press 1987. Copyright © 1987 by Haki Madhubuti. Reprinted by permission of the author.

MAJOR, CLARENCE

Reprinted from *Some Observations of a Stranger at Zuni in the Latter Part of the Century*, Sun & Moon Press "In Hollywood with the Zuni God of War," Copyright © 1989 by Clarence Major. Reprinted by permission of the author.

McCLURE, MICHAEL

"The Death of Kin Cheun Louis." Printed by permission of the author.

McKIM, ELIZABETH

Reprinted from *Boat of the Dream*, "Taking the Name," Copyright © 1988 by Elizabeth McKim; Talking Stone Press, 1988. Reprinted by permission of the author.

MIRIKITANI, JANICE

Reprinted from *Shedding Silence, Poetry and Prose,* Celestial Arts Publishing, "Recipe," "Healthy Choices," "Doreen," "Autumn Comes," "Prisons of Silence," and "Without Tongue," by Janice Mirikitani, Copyright © 1987. Reprinted by permission of the author.

MONTOYA, JOSÉ

"The Uniform of the Day," "Hispanic Nightlife at Luna's Cafe," and "A Chicano Veterano's War Journal," reprinted from *In Formation: 20 Years at Joda,* ed. Arturo Villarreal, Copyright © 1992 by José Montoya. Used by permission of Chusma House.

OATES, JOYCE CAROL

"There was A Shot" appeared in *Western Humanities Review.* Copyright © 1990 by Joyce Carol Oates. Reprinted by permission of the author.

OKITA, DWIGHT

Reprinted from *Crossing With the Light,* "The Nice Thing About Counting Stars" by Dwight Okita; Chicago: Tia Chucha Press, 1992. Copyright © 1992 by Dwight Okita. Reprinted by permission of the author.

OLDS, SHARON

"Leaving the Island" appeared in *The Quarterly* and "The End of World War One" appeared in *The Massachusetts Review.* Copyright © 1979 and 1992 by Sharon Olds. Reprinted by permission of the author.

ORESICK, PETER

Reprinted from *Definitions,* "Poem for Hamid" published by West End Press, Copyright © 1990 by Peter Oresick. Reprinted by permission of the author.

OSTRIKER, ALICIA

"The Leaf Pile" is reprinted from *The Mother/Child Papers,* Beacon Press, 1986, Copyright © 1980 by Alicia Suskin Ostriker. Reprinted by permission of Beacon Press. "The Boys, The Broomhandle, the Retarded Girl" Copyright © 1993 by Alicia Suskin Ostriker. Printed by permission of the author.

PIETRI, PEDRO

Reprinted from *Puerto Rican Obituary,* "Beware of Signs" by Pedro Pietri, Copyright © 1973 by Pedro Pietri. Reprinted by permission of Monthly Review Foundation.

RODRIGUEZ, LUIS J.

Reprinted from *Poems Across the Pavement,* "'Race' Politics" and "Overtown 1984" Copyright © 1989 by Luis J. Rodriguez; Tia Chucha Press, 1989. Reprinted by permission of Tia Chucha Press.

RUDMAN, MARK

Reprinted from *The Nowhere Steps,* "Bottles," sections I, II, III, and IV, Copyright © 1990 by Mark Rudman, The Sheep Meadow Press. Reprinted by permission of the author.

SHAPIRO, HARVEY

Reprinted from *Battle Report,* "How Many Times" by Harvey Shapiro, Wesleyan University Press. Copyright © 1988 by Harvey Shapiro. Reprinted by permission of the author.

SILKO, LESLIE MARMON

Leslie Marmon Silko, author of the essay entitled "The Fourth World," which is to be published as part of a work entitled *Scars: American Poetry in the Face of Violence,* edited by Cynthia Dubin Edelberg, does hereby transfer one-time rights use to the above essay to the University of Alabama Press. Subsequent use must be renegotiated with the author. It is understood that the author reserves all other rights.

SMITH, DAVE

Reprinted from *Gray Soldiers,* "Leafless Trees, Chickahominy Swamp," Copyright © 1984 by Dave Smith. Reprinted by permission of the author.

STAFFORD, WILLIAM

"Entering History" appeared in *The Nation.* "At the Grave of My Brother: Bomber Pilot" appeared in *The Michigan Quarterly.* Copyright © 1990 by William Stafford. Reprinted by permission of the author.

STERN, GERALD

"The Bull Roarer" appeared in *Poetry.* Copyright © 1988 by Gerald Stern. Reprinted by permission of the author.

WAKOSKI, DIANE

Reprinted from *Emerald Ice: Selected Poems, 1962-1987,* "Wind Secrets," Copyright © 1962 by Diane Wakoski, with the permission of Black Sparrow Press.